The Conquest of the Americas

A Captivating Guide to the Discovery of the New World, European Colonization, and Indigenous Resistance

© Copyright 2023 - All rights reserved.

The content contained within this book may not be reproduced, duplicated, or transmitted without direct written permission from the author or the publisher.

Under no circumstances will any blame or legal responsibility be held against the publisher, or author, for any damages, reparation, or monetary loss due to the information contained within this book, either directly or indirectly.

Legal Notice:

This book is copyright protected. It is only for personal use. You cannot amend, distribute, sell, use, quote, or paraphrase any part, or the content within this book, without the consent of the author or publisher.

Disclaimer Notice:

Please note the information contained within this document is for educational and entertainment purposes only. All effort has been executed to present accurate, up-to-date, reliable, and complete information. No warranties of any kind are declared or implied. Readers acknowledge that the author is not engaging in the rendering of legal, financial, medical, or professional advice. The content within this book has been derived from various sources. Please consult a licensed professional before attempting any techniques outlined in this book.

By reading this document, the reader agrees that under no circumstances is the author responsible for any losses, direct or indirect, that are incurred as a result of the use of the information contained within this document, including, but not limited to, errors, omissions, or inaccuracies.

Free Bonus from Captivating History (Available for a Limited time)

Hi History Lovers!

Now you have a chance to join our exclusive history list so you can get your first history ebook for free as well as discounts and a potential to get more history books for free! Simply visit the link below to join.

Captivatinghistory.com/ebook

Also, make sure to follow us on Facebook, Twitter and Youtube by searching for Captivating History.

Table of Contents

INTRODUCTION: ALL THANKS TO THE RECKLESS FEW 1
CHAPTER 1 – THE COLUMBIAN CROSSOVER 3
CHAPTER 2 – CORTÉS THE CONQUEROR MAKES HIS WAY TO MONTEZUMA 15
CHAPTER 3 – THE LAST DAYS OF MONTEZUMA 24
CHAPTER 4 – THE CONSOLIDATION OF NEW SPAIN 29
CHAPTER 5 – THE PLUNDERING OF PERU 37
CHAPTER 6 – THE END OF THE INCA EMPIRE 45
CHAPTER 7 – THE CONQUEST OF THE REST OF SOUTH AMERICA 51
CHAPTER 8 – THE CONQUEST OF SOUTHWESTERN NORTH AMERICA 57
CHAPTER 9 – THE CONQUEST OF CANADA 61
CHAPTER 10 – THE CONQUEST OF THE EASTERN SEABOARD 66
CHAPTER 11 – FROM SEA TO SHINING SEA: THE TAMING OF THE WEST 73
CONCLUSION: THE LEGACY OF THE EUROPEAN CONQUEST 80
HERE'S ANOTHER BOOK BY CAPTIVATING HISTORY THAT YOU MIGHT LIKE 83
FREE BONUS FROM CAPTIVATING HISTORY (AVAILABLE FOR A LIMITED TIME) 84
APPENDIX A: FURTHER READING AND REFERENCE 85

Introduction: All Thanks to the Reckless Few

The Americas, in particular, the United States of America, is often presented as a shining beacon of hope and freedom. Considering the problems that have beset many other parts of the globe, this probably should not come as too much of a surprise. The United States, despite having some of its own issues, has stood tall as a free democratic country of great diversity and strength for many years.

However, the fact that the American continents eventually provided a platform for greatness should not discount the fact that this land was not free for the taking or that the Europeans of the past grabbed it with no opposition. If we were honest about it, we would have to admit that the lands of modern-day North America and South America were seized in bloody conflicts from those who already resided there. Ever since Christopher Columbus landed in the Caribbean, a chain reaction of events occurred, and most of it was not too good for the local inhabitants.

Even when the Europeans made allies with local tribes, it was usually for their own benefit and had the side effect of inflicting the natives with disease, hard labor, or the wrath of their indigenous neighbors. One way or another, the European invaders were hellbent on both dividing and conquering the new lands they found themselves in.

Yes, life typically was not easy for those who were on the conquering end of the conquistadors. But even so, it would be wrong to say there was no benefit whatsoever for those whose lives were transformed by the conquest of the Americas.

Those who lived in the neighboring villages of the Aztec Empire in Mexico must have been relieved when Aztec human sacrifices came to an end. The poor villagers more than likely found themselves laboring hard under a Spanish hacienda, but at least they would not have to fear having their hearts ripped out and their bodies thrown down the bloody steps of an Aztec temple!

So, yes, while the world must openly admit to the trespasses that occurred during the conquest of the Americas, we should not demonize every single aspect of the encounter. For where human beings are present, great shows of compassion and humanity are just as possible as great shows of tyranny and outright oppression. After all, we are dealing with people, and people can display the full gamut of human emotions and experiences at any given time. Friends can become foes, and foes can become friends. In such an uncertain world, it is often the gambler who is able to make quick and decisive decisions at a moment's notice to come out on top.

And those who engaged in the early conquest of the Americas were indeed gamblers of the highest order. They risked life and limb to sail thousands of miles on the high seas to get to the Americas. Once there, they charged ahead into an unknown land, having absolutely no idea what awaited them.

Ironically, one of the most notorious conquistadors, Hernán Cortés, is said to have been a gambling addict. Both his penchant for gambling and womanizing got him into some trouble on the island of Hispaniola just prior to his conquest of the Aztec Empire. It seems that when Hernán Cortés was not storming into ancient temples, he was likely sitting down at a table playing a game of cards (no doubt betting some of that Aztec gold).

Their conquest has been criticized, but one cannot help but admire the sheer audacity of these bold souls who dared to push the envelope and put their lives on the line. It is all thanks to a few reckless adventurers, explorers, conquistadors, and, yes, all-out gamblers who dared to go where no one else would that history has these harrowing tales to tell.

Chapter 1 – The Columbian Crossover

"After having dispatched a meal, I went ashore, and found no habitation save a single house, and that without an occupant. We had no doubt that the people had fled in terror at our approach—as the house was completely furnished."

-*Christopher Columbus*

In the fateful year of 1492, the man who would unwittingly become the vanguard of European conquest—Christopher Columbus—sailed the ocean blue. Contrary to popular belief, he was not setting out to find a new continent. He was simply trying to find an alternative route to India. The traditional land route to the Indian subcontinent had become perilous ever since the Ottoman Turks toppled the city of Constantinople in 1453.

Constantinople (now Istanbul), situated in modern-day Turkey, had formerly been the capital of the eastern half of the Roman Empire. This Roman successor state had hung on for several centuries after the fall of the Western Roman Empire and provided ready access to the East. Traders and merchants could cross Byzantine territory in Asia Minor to reach the lands of the East and the West. But with the defeat of the Byzantines, the Silk Road (which was not one huge highway but rather a bunch of routes connecting the East to the West) was largely shut down.

It was thus of paramount importance for Westerners to find another means of gaining access to the lucrative markets of the East. And this was precisely what Christopher Columbus was attempting to do when he bumped into a large landmass that would later be dubbed "America." Columbus had decided that since the world was round, he could sail west from the Iberian Peninsula and run into India.

The idea is not a bad one—if only Earth was a much smaller place without huge landmasses in between destinations. Instead of sailing straight across the waters and finding India, Christopher Columbus and his crew found something else entirely. Columbus and his men bumped into an unknown set of continents (at least to the Europeans) that would later be dubbed America.

To be clear, Columbus did not discover all of the Americas. He also was not the first European to discover land west of Europe; that honor belongs to Leif Erikson. However, that knowledge was not widely accessible to the broader European continent, and Columbus's discovery should be recognized since his findings brought about the conquest of the Americas.

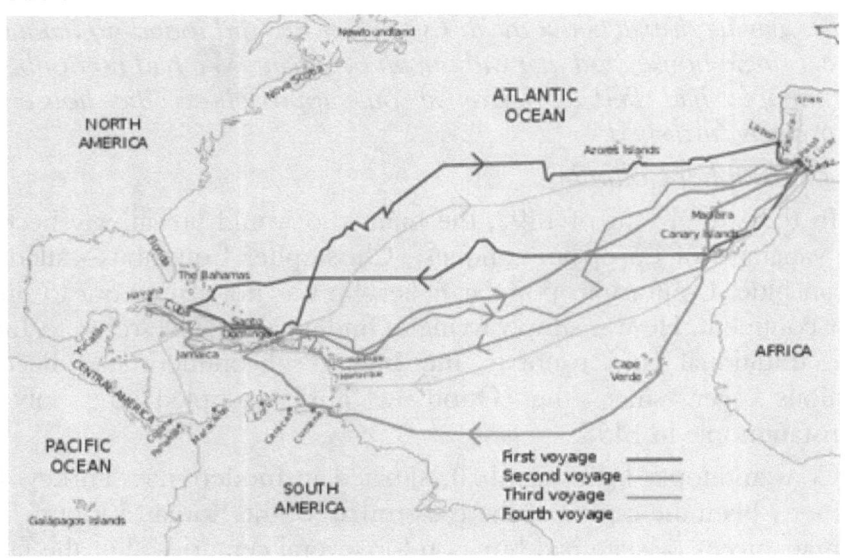

A map of Columbus's voyages to the Americas.
Viajes_de_colon.svg: Phirosiberiaderivative work: Phirosiberia, CC BY-SA 3.0 <https://creativecommons.org/licenses/by-sa/3.0>, via Wikimedia Commons; https://commons.wikimedia.org/wiki/File:Viajes_de_colon_en.svg

Columbus primarily explored the Caribbean, Central America, and South America. In the fall of 1492, Columbus and his men made landfall in the Bahamas. Here, they encountered a local tribe called the

Taíno people, an Arawak subgroup. Since Columbus believed he was in India, he famously misidentified them as "Indians." That name stuck for quite a while; it was only in the 1960s that a big push was made in the United States to use a different term.

The Taíno people proved to be quite friendly and even aided Columbus in finding the biggest chunk of the Caribbean Island chain, Cuba. Shortly thereafter, Columbus traveled southward to what is now Haiti and then on to the Dominican Republic, both of which are part of the island of Hispaniola. It was here that Columbus would be pleased to find gold.

Columbus had his own reasons for exploring the world, but he knew that gold would help finance his expeditions. The supplies and maintenance of the ships were not free, and in order to convince the Spanish monarchs to back his journeys, Columbus needed to be able to promise them some sort of return on their investment; the gold he found on Hispaniola held out the promise to do just that. Columbus returned to Spain with gold, as well as a few locals, and managed to pique the curiosity of the Crown of Castile and Aragon enough for King Ferdinand and Queen Isabella to finance further missions.

Although Columbus would infamously force native inhabitants to mine gold for him, Isabella took the precautionary step of banning slavery. It is certainly arguable what good it might have done, but in the year 1500, Isabella outlawed the enslavement of Native Americans.

We use the term "Native Americans" in retrospect, of course. After all, Columbus thought he was dealing with native islanders in the Indian Ocean. He had no idea that he had landed on the doorstep of another continent.

Nevertheless, even as it was still trying to be determined just what Columbus had "discovered," the Spanish monarchs granted him financing for a few more missions. Columbus would perish a short time later in the year 1506. Columbus would never fully understand what he had discovered. The notion that a new continent could be claimed for Spain would not fully crystalize until shortly after Columbus's demise.

Portugal, in the meantime, would have its own set of explorers basically crash-land in the Americas in 1500. In that year, Portuguese navigator Pedro Álvares Cabral made landfall on what would become known as Brazil. He landed on this northeastern chunk of the South American continent accidentally when his ship was blown off course.

By this time, the Portuguese had already mastered the technique of reaching India by way of circumnavigating the tip of Africa. This method involved sailing south of Portugal toward northwest Africa before heading farther west to get caught up in the powerful westerlies, which would rapidly propel the ship caught in it toward the tip of the African continent. The Portuguese would then sail around the southern tip of Africa and head to India. The trick usually worked like a charm, but on this occasion, Cabral apparently sailed a bit too deep into the westerlies. Instead of being propelled south toward the southern tip of Africa, he was blown farther west to South America.

While in this new land, Cabral and his compatriots noted the abundance of a special kind of red wood, which they called "pau brasil." Brazil got its name from this wood. The Portuguese king would be informed of the find, but Portugal would not make any serious effort to settle the uncharted region until the 1530s.

In the meantime, the Spanish were making some major inroads in the Caribbean. The island of Hispaniola became a major outpost, and many new crops, such as wheat, rice, and onions, among others, were introduced by Spanish settlers.

Beasts of burden, such as donkeys, oxen, goats, and horses, were also introduced. Such things would all be part of the so-called Columbian exchange, which would see Old World items from Europe exchanged for New World items from the Americas.

And thanks to navigator Amerigo Vespucci, who made several groundbreaking forays along the coasts of the Americas in the early 1500s, it was finally realized that a new continent had been discovered. Yes, history got the name "America" from the man who solved the puzzle that Christopher Columbus could not crack.

Amerigo Vespucci "waking up" America.
https://commons.wikimedia.org/wiki/File:%22America%22_(Engraving)_Nova_reperta_(Speculum_diuersarum_imaginum_speculatiuarum_1638).tif

After this realization, a steady campaign of Spanish conquest and colonization began in earnest. In 1508, Cuba had been successfully circumnavigated, and in 1515, Cuba's capital city of Havana was founded.

The Spaniards fought bloody battles to take the island of Puerto Rico in 1509. They had been informed by friendly Taíno inhabitants that a vicious cannibalistic tribe known as the Caribs lived on this island. The conquistadors often sought a pretext for conquest, and they decided this was more than enough of a reason to wage war against the locals. Conquistador Ponce de León led this fight with his trusty and fierce dog Becerrillo at his side.

Interestingly enough, these early inhabitants of what would one day be called Puerto Rico had apparently never seen an attack dog like this before and were absolutely terrified of the animal. They seemed to think he was some sort of mythical beast who could sense their presence through his mystical powers. In reality, the dog just caught their scent and led his handlers to their prey.

The conquistadors fully realized the fear that the dog caused. The animal was sometimes used to intimidate the locals outside of warfare.

However, in one alleged account, the dog seemed to get the better of his handlers.

One day, a rather cold-hearted Spaniard attempted to sic the dog on a local woman. It has been said that the dog simply sniffed her and moved on. Supposedly when Ponce de León got wind of this event, he decided to give the local woman clemency from whatever charges had been made against her while reprimanding his subordinates for their cruelty. According to legend, Ponce de León stated, "I will not allow the compassion and clemency of a dog to overshadow those of a real Christian."

Becerrillo loomed large before the locals. And it was not just because he was a big and fierce dog. The dog was thought to have magical qualities. His ability to find his targets through scent seemed almost magic, as did the fact that he appeared impervious to most arrows.

Native archers often targeted the dog but were dismayed to find that their arrows did not stop him. This was not due to magic; it was due to the effective padded vest that the Spaniards put on the dog. Yes, as much as we might think it funny to put clothing on animals today, such as that snazzy Christmas sweater sported by your local labradoodle, the Spaniards also dressed up their dogs. Well, they dressed them up for war.

It is interesting to note how Puerto Rico has long had legends about mythical beasts with supernatural powers, including stories about the chupacabra, which emerged in the 1990s. At any rate, the conquistadors' dogs did not have any special powers; they were trained to distinguish between the natives' scent and the Spaniards'.

Ponce de León's dog, which was so feared and hated by the locals, would be killed before the conflict was over. But besides killing a conquistador's dog, the Caribs were not able to do much substantial damage to their foes. They folded very quickly, and this Caribbean island became a Spanish possession. From their base in the Caribbean, the Spaniards would launch further forays into the American mainland, making landfall in Mexico, Central America, South America, and even Florida.

In Mesoamerica, unlike their encounters in the Caribbean with loosely connected tribes of hunters and gatherers, the Spanish would come into contact with already established and advanced indigenous civilizations. They would encounter the complex societies of the Maya,

Aztecs, and Incas. Let us start in 1519 when a determined expedition of Spaniards led by Hernán Cortés made its way to Mexico.

Hernán Cortés, who was around thirty years old at the time, was just one of the Spanish explorers. At this point in his career, there was nothing much that distinguished him from his peers. Yet he would soon face off with a great and mighty emperor, the Aztec ruler Montezuma (also spelled as Moctezuma).

The plan to reach the Aztec leader first emerged soon after Cortés landed in the Yucatán. Shortly after he and his crew arrived, they were hailed by a distressed and excited Spaniard named Gerónimo de Aguilar. Gerónimo had first made his way to the region in 1511 when he and his companions encountered another indigenous civilization—the Maya.

It is important to note that although the Maya civilization did exist at the time of the Spanish conquest, it was a mere shadow of what it had once been. For reasons that still remain unknown, the great Maya cities were abandoned around the year 900. After this point, the Maya existed in much smaller, disconnected communities throughout the Yucatán.

Although the Maya were small players compared to the Aztecs in the early 1500s, a band of Maya encountered Gerónimo. Gerónimo and his compatriots' ship had wrecked, and they were in need of assistance. The Maya, however, sensed trouble and quickly seized the strange visitors as prisoners.

The reactions of the Maya are important to contemplate because they were far different from how the Aztecs and Incas would later respond. Considering what happened to the Aztecs and Incas, one might consider the standoffish yet proactive stance of the Maya to be prudent, perhaps even wise.

The Maya kept careful watch of their prisoners of war; it was as if they were deeply concerned about what might happen should their charges escape. Did they know something others did not? Did they realize these strangers could bring about the collapse of entire civilizations if left unchecked?

Nevertheless, Gerónimo managed to get away from his captors, and he told Cortés and company his tale. He claimed that some of his former compatriots had been slaughtered in a ritual human sacrifice. The tales of the locals engaging in human sacrifice were met with disgust, and the Spaniards would use such things as a pretext for their conquest of the Aztecs.

It is important to note that Hernán Cortés was not the first Spanish conquistador to embark upon a major expedition in the region. Francisco Córdoba had attempted to make major inroads in the Yucatán a couple of years prior to Hernán Cortés in 1517, but he and his group largely met with failure. The Córdoba expedition set sail from Cuba on February 8th, 1517, and after getting caught in a terrible storm, they sailed west and managed to make landfall on the Yucatán.

Soon after they made landfall, the explorers saw a large stone structure—a pyramid—that seemed to jut up out of the trees in the distance. As they moved farther up the coast, they came across the outskirts of a town made up of sturdy stone dwellings.

The Spaniards were startled to see ten big canoes pull up alongside their vessels. The two parties apparently got a good look at each other before they attempted communication with rudimentary gestures of their hands. The Spaniards were able to convey warm wishes well enough to get the leader of the group and several of his men to agree to step aboard their craft. Both parties engaged in further gestures of goodwill, and the chief was given a gift of green glass beads.

The Spaniards were used to giving trinkets to locals they encountered. It was not uncommon for the Spanish to trade glass beads for silver and gold. In fact, Hernán Cortés, prior to his arrival in the Yucatán, successfully gained the support of locals on the island of Cozumel, just east of the Yucatán, in a very similar fashion.

At any rate, the Maya that Córdoba encountered seemed pleased enough with the gesture. The Maya party communicated they had to depart but that they would return the following day. Due to the goodwill between the two groups, the Spaniards felt assured enough to set anchor and call it a night.

The next morning, an even larger group of Maya, led by the same chief, greeted them. The chief insisted that the Spanish come ashore so that he could show them around. Córdoba accepted the chief's friendly gestures. Córdoba and his crew were led to the chief's village, which was nestled fairly deep in the wilderness of the interior. When they reached a clearing, the chief betrayed them. It was a trap, and as soon as the chief called out in a loud voice, a vast number of Maya warriors waiting to ambush the strangers leaped out of the shadows.

The Spaniards were being made into target practice as Maya arrows fired with fury at their mailed forms. The first wave of this onslaught was terrible. The Maya managed to kill fifteen of Córdoba's men. The Spanish were able to rally, and upon taking evasive action, Spanish swords, armor, and guns were able to gain the upper hand slowly but surely. Despite the fact the Spaniards were greatly outnumbered, the Maya, weary of being hacked into pieces by Spanish steel and terrified by the blasts of Spanish guns, decided to abandon the assault.

This opened the way for the Spaniards to advance to one of the great stone temples they had beheld from the coast. They found the place unguarded and full of gold idols. The Spanish quickly snatched up the idols before storming back through the wilderness and boarding their ships. Córdoba and his men would later face another attack (maybe someone was a bit unhappy that the temple had been looted), and he would not get away so easily.

Outnumbered by a large contingent of Maya, Córdoba would receive a fatal wound in a battle. Many of his men also died. Despite the heavy losses Córdoba and his crew sustained, this glimpse of tantalizing riches in the mainland of the Americas would spur more conquistadors to explore and conquer. Hernán Cortés was a part of these follow-up expeditions. When he befriended the former prisoner of the Maya, Gerónimo, Cortés realized he had found a key to unlock the conquest of the mainland.

The freed Gerónimo proved to be quite useful in expeditions since he had picked up the Mayan language. He was responsible for engaging in dialogue with the locals as the Spaniards made their way farther inland. Gerónimo proved to be an asset in early March of 1519 when the Spanish expedition reached the outskirts of the town of Tabasco and found their way blocked by a large contingent of warriors.

Gerónimo Aguilar was dispatched to send a message to the chief in charge to see why their path was blocked. The chief's message was clear: the Spaniards were trespassing, and if they did not leave immediately, they would have to do battle. Hernán Cortés was smart enough to pick and choose his battles carefully. He was not ready to face off against thousands of warriors, so he heeded the warning and ordered his troops to fall back.

This was only a brief diversion. On March 13th, Hernán Cortés and his men were already preparing for a renewed confrontation. He assembled a group of some one hundred troops and sent them to face the thousands of warriors that were blocking their path. However, before hostilities ensued, the Spaniards were obligated to read the locals the Requerimiento or, as it is in English, the "Requirement."

Those who were on the verge of being conquered were supposed to be told that if they accepted Christ and acknowledged the authority of both the pope and the king of Spain, they would be spared, and there would be no need for war. As many scholars have pointed out, most of the indigenous inhabitants of the New World had no way of understanding much of any of this. Even with the aid of Gerónimo translating the words of the Requerimiento into the Mayan tongue, it typically struck those who heard it as entirely absurd. Christian beliefs were foreign to them, and they did not know these foreign leaders; it made no sense for them to bow down to them.

Cortés most likely assumed that the obligatory Requerimiento would be rejected, but reading the locals "their rights" likely gave him the solace of following the king's decree and justifying what would happen. Cortés was ready to wage an all-out war on those who stood in opposition to him.

After the Requerimiento was read, the Maya executed the first wave of their attack, which consisted of sending canoes full of warriors who let loose a multitude of arrows on Hernán Cortés and his troops. The warriors on land then rushed in, and the two sides fought what at first appeared to be a bloody stalemate. The outnumbered Spaniards were eventually able to leverage their advantage of steel swords, armor, and guns and push back their opponents, who sustained heavy losses.

The Tabasco warriors who dared block the path of the Spaniards fled the town and ran for the hills. Practically all of the inhabitants of Tabasco followed suit. The victorious Spaniards then set up shop right in the middle of the deserted town of Tabasco. Hernán Cortés went to the trouble of dispatching five prisoners of war—Tabasco warriors who had just been captured—to inform their tribal leaders that he wished to come to some sort of understanding.

These were attempts at peaceful overtures to be sure, but since the chiefs were never likely to agree to the Requerimiento, the efforts were destined to be futile. Nevertheless, once it was clear there would be no acceptance of his overtures, Hernán Cortés marched his troops out of the town and caught the native forces by surprise by charging them headlong and pushing them out into the open. The Tabasco warriors' main strategy was to overtake the Spaniards with brute, overwhelming force.

The Spanish lines began to buckle under the strain of this deluge of warriors; it seemed to everyone involved the Spanish troops might be on the verge of defeat. The only thing that saved the day was Cortés calling in the calvary. Just as the Spanish infantry was on the verge of collapse, Hernán Cortés led Spanish armored soldiers on horseback right into the enemy lines.

Their opponents had never dealt with horses before, and the sight of an armored Spaniard on an armored horse was frightening and disorienting. After the rapid charge left countless trampled by horse hooves and butchered by steel swords, the Tabasco warriors panicked and broke into a disorderly retreat. Subsequent overtures to the defeated natives would lead to a more conciliatory response.

In their efforts to appease the victors, the indigenous people began presenting them with some consolation prizes. Locals began to arrive at the Spaniards' camp, loaded with valuable gold ornaments. Also among them were several indigenous women offered up as slaves to the Spaniards. One of these women, whom the Spaniards would later call Doña Marina, was an Aztec known as La Malinche.

She spoke both Mayan and the Aztec language (Nahuatl). Doña Marina was a quick study, and with Gerónimo's help, she was soon able to add Spanish to her list of languages. Doña Marina would then be able to translate the Aztec and Mayan languages into Spanish for the Spaniards, and she could dutifully relay their responses back to the Aztecs and Maya.

The Spaniards would rely upon her as their translator for the rest of their expedition. And Doña Maria would indeed prove to be the key to the Spanish conquest of what would become known as Mexico. In modern-day Mexico, popular opinion of this figure is typically split. Some view her as a saint, while others think she was the worst of traitors.

At any rate, with the loyal Doña Marina in tow, the entourage of Hernán Cortés and his conquistadors made their way through Aztec territory. They would meet with various tribal leaders, exchange gifts, and establish important contacts along the way. Eventually, they came in contact with direct emissaries of the powerful Aztec leader Montezuma, who showered the Spaniards with gifts while attempting to probe their true intentions.

Before making contact with Montezuma, Hernán Cortés would set up a valuable outpost on the Mexican mainland by building a port city he called Vera Cruz. This settlement would be crucial since this hub could provide an outlet to Cuba, allowing reinforcements and goods to be sent back and forth.

In November 1519, Hernán Cortés and his group of conquistadors chosen for the expedition reached the outskirts of Montezuma's great capital. The Aztec capital city of Tenochtitlan was unparalleled both in the Americas and much of the rest of the world at the time.

The city was massive and built in a lake, with causeways stretching out on all sides. It was a nearly impregnable fortress, and it would have been very difficult to have taken from the outside. The thing is, Cortés would not have to. He would use guile and deception to connive his way right into Montezuma's courts, which allowed him to betray the Aztec monarch from within his own city.

Chapter 2 – Cortés the Conqueror Makes His Way to Montezuma

"Thus they have an idol that they petition for victory in war; another for success in their labors; and so for everything in which they seek or desire prosperity, they have their idols, which they honor and serve."

-Hernán Cortés

By the fall of 1519, the Aztec ruler Montezuma had learned of the strangers that were headed toward his capital city of Tenochtitlan. His scribes had encountered them and had even sketched drawings of Spanish soldiers in armor and their majestic and frightening steeds. Before any of the Spaniards even arrived in the capital, Montezuma's court was abuzz with what all of this might mean.

Montezuma spoke with his advisors at great length about these strange developments, and somewhere along the line, a theory was hatched that the leader of these interlopers—Hernán Cortés—might be the prophesized return of the Aztec deity Quetzalcoatl. The Aztecs had a legend of a great and wise teacher who had traveled across the sea and bestowed his knowledge upon the Aztecs before heading back east over the sea from where he had come.

It was prophesized that the great Quetzalcoatl would return someday. When it was learned that these strange men had come from the east, some wondered if Quetzalcoatl might be among them or if these figures were representatives of Quetzalcoatl.

To be clear, it is not certain that Montezuma himself ever really believed that Hernán Cortés was Quetzalcoatl. At the very least, Montezuma felt that Hernán Cortés and his associates were unusual visitors and sought to figure out as much as possible about them before making any decision on what to do with them.

When Montezuma sent another entourage bearing gifts, Cortés's personal translator, Doña Marina, grasped what was going on. By picking up snatches of conversation from the courtiers, she realized there was a rumor afoot that Hernán Cortés might be the returned Quetzalcoatl. Doña Marina allegedly informed Cortés of this fact. The cunning woman also encouraged him to play to their beliefs to take advantage of the superstitions of Montezuma's court. It is for this reason—at least according to some accounts—that Doña Marina, more commonly known as La Malinche among modern-day Mexicans, is often perceived as a traitor.

Cortés took Doña Marina (La Malinche) up on her advice and began playing up his supposed role as Quetzalcoatl.

Even so, Montezuma continued to delay when Cortés asked for an official audience with him. Ultimately, Hernán Cortés decided to force his hand. He led his troops farther inland, where they met and befriended the Totonac tribe, which was a subject tributary of the Aztecs. The Totonac people had to pay tribute not only in treasure but also in humans for the constant human sacrifices that were carried out in the Aztec capital of Tenochtitlan.

The Spaniards saw an example of this demand for sacrificial victims being played out when Aztec "tax collectors" arrived to collect their human tribute. Hernán Cortés managed to convince those he had recently befriended to rebel against the Aztecs, and the startled tax collectors of Montezuma were suddenly seized by the Totonac tribe, who were being promised the support of Spanish arms.

This first rebellion against Aztec rule would ripple through the fabric of the Aztec Empire, and Montezuma would soon hear about it from his perch in Tenochtitlan. Nevertheless, Montezuma still hesitated to act.

In the meantime, Hernán Cortés gained more allies, and by August, he had picked up the support of the powerful Tlaxcala people, who had long been a troublesome thorn in the side of the Aztecs. The Spanish did not gain the trust of the Tlaxcala until a contingent of Spanish troops defeated a large number of them in battle. As was typical, the Spaniards were greatly outnumbered in this exchange, but Spanish steel and military tactics were able to win the day. After this conflict, the Tlaxcala decided that the military might of the Spaniards might provide them with the opportunity they were looking for to throw off the Aztec yoke once and for all.

After a series of lengthy discussions between representatives of the Tlaxcala and Hernán Cortés, an allegiance was agreed to. At this point, Cortés and his troops were being significantly bolstered by their native auxiliaries. And while Cortés's entourage of supporters continued to grow, the Spanish continued to make their way eve to Tenochtitlan. Montezuma was well aware of these happenings and sent out emissaries, who invited Hernán Cortés to pay a visit to the town of Cholula, which rested just at the gates of Tenochtitlan.

Hernán Cortés was warned by his Tlaxcalan guides this was likely a trap. He was told the Aztecs were often duplicitous in their dealings and that there would almost certainly be a contingent of Aztec warriors waiting to ambush Cortés and his troops if they showed their faces in Cholula. Nevertheless, trap or no trap, Cortés was determined to go forward, so he took the Aztecs up on their invitation and made his way to Cholula.

The Cholula were not so easily swayed to the side of the Spaniards, but they were pragmatic enough to know not to arouse their wrath. As such, they played it safe and made an appearance of appeasement while secretly sending their own emissaries to Montezuma to alert the Aztecs of what was transpiring. Meanwhile, Cortés and his men were allowed to camp out in the courtyard of one of the main temples in the town.

As they awaited word from Tenochtitlan, Doña Marina learned from one of the locals that the Cholulans were actively colluding with the Aztecs to ambush the Spaniards. The plot would have had the Cholulan guides turn on the Spaniards as they led them to Tenochtitlan. There would also be a force of tens of thousands of Aztec fighters waiting to descend upon them. If this plan had been executed, even Spanish steel likely would not have been enough for the Spanish to emerge victorious.

However, Cortés found out about the Chululans' duplicity and confronted a group of Cholulan nobles about it. The nobles adamantly denied that any plot was in the works, but Hernán Cortés insisted that he knew about what they had planned and outlined the plot in such detail that the nobles themselves could hardly deny it.

They eventually came clean and admitted their role in the conspiracy. After admitting as much, they begged Cortés for mercy, insisting that since they had been ordered by Montezuma to carry out this scheme, they did not have much say in the matter. But Cortés was not in the mood for mercy and instead enacted a bloody reprisal against them. Utilizing a prearranged signal of firing a gun into the air, the Spaniards, along with their indigenous allies, began letting loose on every Cholulan in sight.

Thousands would be dead before Hernán Cortés gave the order to end the bloodbath. After the massacre was over, Cortés summoned the surviving chiefs and informed them he was willing to offer his forgiveness for their betrayal. He informed them that they would be allowed to continue with their lives peacefully and that he would keep his men and native allies from doing them any further harm.

Cortés also managed to insert religion into the discussion. He insisted that he knew what had occurred was not completely their fault since they were clearly under the deceptive power of false gods. Cortés insisted that if they turned to Christ and forgot their old religion, their deception would leave them, and they would be fully rehabilitated. Cortés then tore down idols that had been in Cholulan temples and had Christian crosses erected in their place. He also put an end to human sacrifice, freeing those who had been locked up in wooden cages and consigned to annihilation.

Hernán Cortés soon sent a message to Montezuma. In this missive, Cortés did not give any hint of the previous betrayal; instead, he insisted that he have an audience with the great Aztec leader. Aztec dignitaries were sent to Cholula to speak with Cortés. Montezuma apparently wished to play the consolation card now that the ambush had been foiled and had his representatives shower Cortés with gifts of gold, ornate clothing, and food.

Montezuma's men also relayed the message that the Aztec king claimed he had nothing to do with the plot. Yes, even while the Cholulan leaders pointed the finger of blame squarely at Tenochtitlan, Montezuma claimed that it was the Cholulans who were entirely at fault. They furthermore issued Montezuma's condolences for what had happened and extended a formal invitation for Hernán Cortés to meet with him in Tenochtitlan.

Hernán Cortés, who was looking for just such an opportunity, readily agreed. Even so, Cortés was not gullible enough to think that Montezuma was really so welcoming. He knew that Montezuma would likely strike out at him and his troops if the opportunity presented itself. As such, during the trek to the Aztec capital, Cortés remained on his guard.

In November 1519, the forces of Hernán Cortés traveled through the Valley of Mexico and reached Lake Texcoco, upon which Tenochtitlan rested. The Spaniards marveled at the majestic bridges that stretched out from the Aztec capital across the lake. One of Cortés's compatriots, Bernal Díaz, documented the sense of wonder they felt.

Díaz would later recall, "Gazing on such wonderful sights, we did not know what to say, or whether what appeared before us was real, for on one side, on the land, there were great cities, and in the lake ever so many more, and the lake itself was crowded with canoes, and in the causeway were many bridges at intervals, and in front of us stood the great city of Mexico."

It is interesting to note that Díaz was already referring to Tenochtitlan offhand as the "great city of Mexico" in light of the fact that the Spaniards would soon dub the place "Mexico City."

Montezuma decided it would be better to meet the interlopers head-on. Cortés and his men soon beheld his arrival. They spotted Montezuma being carried on a golden litter. The Aztec king was brought in front of the Spaniards and gently placed on the ground before he exited the litter. Flanked by his loyal entourage, Montezuma made his way to Cortés.

Montezuma was clearly expecting them. He made no threatening gestures, but he was not completely forthcoming either. Nevertheless, Hernán Cortés was face to face with the great Aztec ruler at last.

Hernán Cortés had Doña Marina at his side, and through her, he carried out a lengthy conversation with Montezuma. He was also given many expensive gifts of gold and jewels. According to some accounts, Cortés learned, through Doña Marina's translation, that Montezuma was under the impression that Hernán Cortés was possibly the fulfillment of the prophecy related to Quetzalcoatl. Hernán Cortés, perhaps with Doña Marina's encouragement, proceeded to indulge Montezuma's fantasies.

Interestingly enough, a part of the legend of Quetzalcoatl spoke of how this deity did not approve of human sacrifice and wished to put a stop to it. It was predicted that he would attempt to end the practice when he returned. The fact that Cortés, as a Christian, abhorred the practice does seem to line up with this aspect of the legend.

Shortly after this exchange, Hernán Cortés was escorted to Montezuma's palace. Here, the conversation continued, and Cortés began to speak of how he represented a mighty faraway ruler named Charles. He was referring to Charles V, who was both the king of Spain (as Charles I) as well as the Holy Roman emperor (as Charles V). Charles V had control of a large swathe of central and western Europe.

If the story of Montezuma believing Cortés to be a god is true, he likely would have been confused at Cortés being a representative of another ruler. The two men clearly had much more to discuss, but it was getting late. Montezuma decided it would be best to retire for the evening and that they could speak further the next day.

Montezuma had his assistants lead Hernán Cortés to the former palace of his father, Axayacatl, where he would be able to rest honorably. The Aztec king then made his way back to his own palace, departing the same way he had come.

In the days that followed their first encounter, Cortés and Montezuma discussed many matters at great length through the help of their interpreters. However, both men, who were steeped in their own personal religious views, could not help but fall back on religious beliefs as a main topic of conversation. Soon enough, Hernán Cortés was giving Montezuma the tried and true "Requerimiento," informing him of the Christian religion and its relationship with the pope and reigning monarch of Spain and the Holy Roman Empire, Charles V.

Montezuma listened intently to what Hernán Cortés had to say, but at every turn, he insisted that the religion of his ancestors was what made Tenochtitlan so great and that continued adherence to the rituals and traditions of the past was necessary. Growing weary of religious discussion, Montezuma decided to lead his guests on a kind of "guided tour" around the city. The Spaniards saw many intriguing sights, the highlight of which seemed to be a kind of zoo that the Aztecs had set up stocked with all kinds of exotic animals.

But the sight that got the Spaniards' attention the most was the bloody temples, which bore the marks of a recent human sacrifice. The

Spaniards had already been made aware of this custom, but now they were face to face with the grisly reality that sacrifices were being carried out on a massive scale. This was also indicated by two huge towers in the middle of the city that were lined with hundreds of human heads taken from some of those unfortunate sacrificial subjects.

The practice was no secret, and Montezuma openly explained that human sacrifice was part of Aztec religious beliefs. Montezuma even led the Spaniards to the temple of the Aztec deity Huitzilopochtli to see some of this practice in action. Cortés and his men were led up the long staircase of the temple into a dark room dimly lit by candles. Here, they came face to face with a giant statue of the ominous Huitzilopochtli.

Scattered around the statue were hearts that had recently been ripped from their hosts and offered as sacrifices. Blood stained the walls and the floors, making the Aztec temple seem more like a butcher house than anything else. Hernán Cortés and his compatriots were taking note of all of this and would use their distaste for this practice as a reason to topple the Aztecs.

For the moment, however, Cortés realized that he would have to play along and bide his time, lest he anger Montezuma and cause him and his allies to be rendered into sacrificial lambs and slaughtered in the Aztec temple. Hernán Cortés was prepared to play the long game, but he soon received tidings that spurred him to act.

Cortés received word that some of the men who had remained behind at Veracruz had been ambushed by the Aztecs. If his soldiers were being attacked farther afield, he realized that his precarious position in the heart of the Aztec Empire was growing more and more uncertain by the minute. It was at this point that he determined that taking Montezuma as a hostage was likely the best chance he had to buy some insurance for the safety of himself and his troops.

He achieved this by inviting Montezuma for yet another of their talks. But it was not religion that Cortés wished to discuss. Instead, he immediately confronted Montezuma with the news of the assault on his troops. Montezuma denied any knowledge of the engagement and promised to have those responsible punished.

Nevertheless, Hernán Cortés managed to corner the Aztec monarch, and as Spanish troops circled around him, Cortés informed the Aztec ruler that he was going to be placed under his own personal custody. It is said that Montezuma apparently submitted to his captors; he likely realized.

The citizens of the city were certainly shocked to see their ruler walking the streets escorted by the Spaniards. Montezuma, apparently fearing a complete disintegration of the social fabric, let it be known that he was fine and that he was in complete control of the situation.

This, of course, was what the Spaniards wanted him to say so that they would have an effective puppet they could vicariously rule through. Testing the limits of his powers, Cortés attempted to throw his weight around by demanding that Montezuma halt Aztec religious practices and convert his people to Christianity.

This was a bridge too far for Montezuma, who insisted that even if he lost his life, there was no way the Aztecs would shed their ancestral worship. Montezuma made it clear that if the Aztec temples were shut down, the Aztecs would rise up as a whole to annihilate the Spanish invaders. Hernán Cortés must have realized that Montezuma was speaking the truth because he settled on a compromise.

Instead of abolishing the Aztec religion outright, Montezuma agreed to halt the human sacrifices that offended Spanish sensibilities. But even this was a compromise within a compromise. Hernán Cortés did not realize that Montezuma was only agreeing to halt human sacrifice within sight of the Spaniards. The practice was allowed to continue away from watching Spanish eyes.

Hernán Cortés pressed the matter of Christianity further and was soon asking for a cross to be placed in the main Aztec temple. Montezuma's priests refused to allow articles of Christian faith to be placed inside the temple and insisted that such a thing could not occur.

Cortés's efforts were interrupted when he learned that even more trouble was afoot on the coast. This time around, the chaos that had erupted had nothing to do with the Aztecs; rather, the problems came from other Spaniards. The Spanish authorities in Cuba did not like what Hernán Cortés was doing in Mexico and sent fellow conquistador Pánfilo de Narváez to disrupt his efforts. At the time, Cortés was considered a renegade who was operating without the official approval of his immediate superior, the governor of Cuba.

Narváez landed on the Mexican coast in order to rectify this situation and began skirmishing with Cortés's troops. Cortés was forced to leave Montezuma and Tenochtitlan in the charge of his subordinates as he rushed back to the coast to lead his men against the forces of Narváez.

It is important to fully understand Cortés's renegade status at the time of his conquests since it helps us to better appreciate the man's mental state at the time. If his expedition in the Americas failed and he was forced to return empty-handed, he faced certain imprisonment and even death at the hands of Spanish authorities.

The fact that Cortés had so thoroughly burned his bridges with no way to return to Cuba unless he was so overladen with gold and glory that his transgressions could be overlooked does much to explain his audacity. For him, it was truly a do-or-die moment.

Before reaching Narváez, Hernán Cortés made a pivotal stop in Tlaxcala, where the troops already at his disposal were bolstered with more Tlaxcalan reinforcements. It was a protracted and bloody struggle, but the Hernán Cortés faction ultimately overcame the forces of Narváez, thereby ensuring that the destruction of the Aztecs would proceed.

Chapter 3 – The Last Days of Montezuma

"The city is as large as Seville or Cordova; its streets, I speak of the principal ones, are very wide and straight, some of these, and all the inferior ones, are half land and half water, and are navigated by canoes."

-*Hernán Cortés*

Upon his return to Tenochtitlan in the summer of 1520, the victorious Hernán Cortés arrived with a force that had been significantly bolstered by Spaniards who had served under Narváez and defected to his side. Cortés promised these men that untold riches awaited them in the conquest of the Aztec Empire; this was apparently enough to persuade them to throw in their lot with Cortés.

Cortés had been away for roughly a month, having left the occupation of the Aztec capital in the hands of Pedro de Alvarado. During the absence of Cortés, Pedro had nearly lost control of the city and had become a virtual prisoner inside one of Montezuma's palaces, where he and his soldiers were holed up.

Rather than being greeted at the gates, Cortés found the metropolis to be strangely quiet. The lake was bereft of the usual canoes, and city thoroughfares that had previously been bustling with activity were empty. Even so, as Hernán Cortés and company made their way to the capital, they could not help but feel the many eyes of the Aztecs watching them.

At any rate, Cortés made his way to the palace-turned-garrison, and after giving Alvarado a good tongue lashing for his many failures, he heaped abuse on Montezuma for supposedly not controlling his subjects. Cortés then ordered Montezuma to speak to his people to get them to come out of hiding and return to the marketplace and other vital functions so the city could return to normal.

However, Montezuma insisted that the people were no longer willing to listen to him and suggested that a noble by the name of Cuitláhuac go in his place. This noble was actually Montezuma's brother. Hernán Cortés agreed to this plan of action, but it would backfire spectacularly when Cuitláhuac went straight to the Aztec deliberative body known as the Great Council and declared that his brother was a puppet of the enemy. Cuitláhuac also declared that from that point forward, he would take over command.

The council agreed and recognized Cuitláhuac as the new Aztec emperor. Shortly thereafter, Cuitláhuac rallied a massive Aztec force and prepared them to rid the city of the Spaniards. Cortés and his followers were once again imprisoned in the Palace of Axayacatl, surrounded on all sides by an ever-growing mob of angry Aztecs. Cortés immediately decided to go on the offensive, sending out some four hundred troops in an attempt to force the Aztecs back with Spanish steel and guns.

But besieged by a multitude of arrows, darts, spears, and rocks, the Spanish troops were forced to give ground, losing several of their men in the process. Ultimately, this contingent of Spaniards was forced to make a run for it, retreating back to the walls of the palace. Even getting back to the palace was no easy feat, and it was only through the aid of Spanish guns being repeatedly fired into the throngs of Aztecs by those already in the palace that the Spaniards on the outside were able to gain entrance.

The fighting was so terrible that it has been said that besides the several slain Spanish soldiers, there was not one from the group who had dared this offensive and managed to escape without some form of injury.

The Aztecs then began to use flaming arrows to set the palace and surrounding area on fire. The Spaniards had no water at their disposal, so they attempted to use handfuls of dirt to snuff out as much of the blaze as they could.

Somehow, the Spanish made it through the night, but the very next morning, the Aztecs resumed their assault, and their numbers appeared to be even more than they had been the previous day. Despite the previously aborted offensive, Hernán Cortés decided that a mad dash out of the palace was their only hope. As such, he rolled the dice and decided that it was an all-or-nothing moment. He led the bulk of his army to try to smash their way through the massive mob.

It was a terrible struggle to fight their way out of the city. Not only were they harried and hounded on all sides by arrows, darts, and stones, but the bridges that led from the capital across the lake had also been purposefully sabotaged. Huge gaps were dug into them, making the crossing extremely difficult. The Spaniards had to improvise where possible, using everything from stone rubble to the dead bodies of their own fallen comrades to make their way across.

It is said that roughly two-thirds of Hernán Cortés's forces perished in this daring escape. After they fought their way out of Tenochtitlan, Cortés and what was left of his army went to the friendly lands of his Tlaxcala allies.

Here, they had some respite and were able to take a breath and attempt to heal their battered bodies. Hernán Cortés himself had received a nearly fatal head injury and lost two fingers. He and his men had survived to see another day but just barely. Cortés and his followers would spend much of the rest of the year recuperating.

By this point, Montezuma was dead. It remains a bit unclear what exactly happened to Montezuma. Some accounts say that he was stoned by his own subjects. It is also possible that the Spanish were behind his death or encouraged the Aztecs to kill him.

Today, the term "Montezuma's Revenge" refers to travel diarrhea that visitors may get when traveling to Mexico. Legend says that Montezuma gave "gringos" diarrhea in revenge for his death and the end of the Aztec culture.

At any rate, the new Aztec emperor, Cuitláhuac, was attempting to rally an even greater force by gaining the support of surrounding tribes. Most of these efforts failed to materialize since many of the surrounding tribes, although not as hostile as the Tlaxcalans, had long been frustrated with the Aztecs due to high taxes and the harsh annual tributes that had been exacted from them.

As such, Cuitláhuac's efforts were not well received. The Aztecs had even worse problems since the scourge of smallpox, a damning legacy of the Spaniards, had begun to take hold. Many, including Cuitláhuac himself, would perish before this terrible contagion ran its course. Cuitláhuac was succeeded by the young Aztec prince Cuauhtémoc.

Hernán Cortés returned to the Aztec capital in 1521, and by April, he was already plying the waters surrounding Tenochtitlan with small boats outfitted with cannons so that he could mercilessly bombard the Aztec capital from the lake. The Aztecs attempted to counteract this bombardment by having Aztec warriors row out in canoes to face this menace. The Aztecs wished to disable the Spanish guns, but they had to get to them first, and such a task certainly was not easy. Many were literally blown out of the water by these makeshift gunboats before they were able to get anywhere near them.

Even so, the incessant waves of Aztecs hampered the progress of the Spanish invasion. It actually was not until June that the Spaniards were able to set foot into the capital city of the Aztec Empire. The Aztec defenders then rallied around the Great Temple in the city center.

The Spaniards seemed to think they had the Aztec warriors on the run and did everything they could to press their advantage. But as soon as they approached the Great Temple, Aztecs hidden on the roofs of surrounding buildings began to hurl arrows, rocks, and other debris down on the Spaniards. To put a stop to these ambush attacks from on high, Hernán Cortés ordered his men to set fire to the city.

Buildings were set ablaze, and the tactic did seem to slow the Aztecs down, but it did not prevent the Spaniards from suffering heavy losses. This was evidenced when several Spaniards were captured and later used as sacrifices in the Aztec temple. These men were made examples of, with their hearts being ripped out of their chests and their lifeless bodies tossed down the temple steps. This sacrificial ceremony was performed right in the midst of this immense struggle.

At one point, Hernán Cortés was knocked off his horse and very nearly captured. If it was not for the heroics of Cristóbal de Olea, who rushed over to rescue the fallen conquistador, the conquest of Mexico likely would have turned out much differently. Instead of toppling an empire, Cortés likely would have been yet another sacrificial victim of the Aztec religion.

As it were, Cristóbal was able to dash to Cortés's side just as eager hands were threatening to drag him away. Cristóbal used his sword to chop off an arm that belonged to one of those eager hands.

As dreadful as all of this was, Hernán Cortés was now playing the long game. He knew that he had this city under siege and that as its food and water supplies ran low, so would the morale of the city's defenders.

On August 13th, 1521, the Aztec resistance finally gave up the ghost. Aztec defenses had been thoroughly demolished, and countless warriors were dead. No longer able to muster a significant force, Aztec Emperor Cuauhtémoc attempted to escape across the lake by canoe as the last ember of resistance was snuffed out.

However, there was no way the Spanish would let him get away, and as soon as he was spotted fleeing the scene, he was seized and placed under the custody of the Spaniards. He would languish as a prisoner for a few more years before he was executed in 1525. The Aztec Empire was no more.

From the ashes of Tenochtitlan, a new capital would rise. Thanks to Hernán Cortés and his followers, the Aztec world of old had come to an end. It is interesting to note that the Aztecs long feared that any cessation of their ritualized human sacrifices would trigger the end of the world, and in a way, it did.

Earth might have kept spinning, but one could say that the Aztec world as they knew it came to a grinding halt. The new city constructed in the heart of the Valley of Mexico would simply be called Mexico City, and the larger surrounding region would be known as Mexico.

Chapter 4 – The Consolidation of New Spain

"And after I rallied with the horsemen, I turned on them [the K'iches], and here a very severe pursuit and punishment was made. In this affair one of the four chiefs of the city of Utatlan was killed, who was captain general of all this country. I returned to the spring and there made camp for the night, greatly fatigued, and with several Spaniards and horses wounded."

-Pedro de Alvarado

In the immediate aftermath of the conquest of the Aztec Empire, Hernán Cortés fired off a missive to King Charles V of Spain and the Holy Roman Empire, detailing the defeat of the Aztecs and the securing of Mexico. Soon, settlers, both those who were already in the Caribbean and fresh faces from Spain, would come pouring into the former lands of the Aztec Empire.

This flood of immigrants was likely one of the greatest shocks of all to the conquered inhabitants. They had just suffered a defeat at the hands of a few hundred Spaniards, but they had no idea that more of them were on their way. They most likely figured that the Spanish who were already there would either lord over them as rulers or even take all of their gold and depart.

No one quite realized that these strange visitors were playing for keeps and would put down roots so they could superimpose their culture, language, and religion throughout the land. As shocking as the changes must have been, it was not all bad for everyone. It has been noted that much of the Aztec nobility was left intact, and lands and special privileges remained in place as long as the noble classes dutifully converted to Christianity.

This, of course, was part of the Spaniards' two-pronged effort of conversion, which used both incentives as well as punishment to coerce the natives to conform to Catholic religious dogma. But perhaps the factor that played into the transformation of Mexico more than anything else was the rapid pace of intermarriage that took place between the Spanish and the indigenous peoples of Mexico.

These unions, which were actively encouraged by the Catholic Church, created a new generation of Mexicans known as mestizos in a very short period of time. According to Central American chronicler Lynn Foster, who has documented these developments, Central America currently boasts a mestizo population of 62 percent.

The man who was the most pivotal in bringing all of this about, Hernán Cortés, was celebrated by most Spaniards as a hero. He had boldly marched into these strange lands and forever left Spain's mark on the New World. Today, the indigenous lands of Mexico and Guatemala seem just about inseparable from the undercurrents of the Spanish language and culture, and we, for better or worse, largely have Cortés to blame for that.

Cortés has largely been vilified in modern discourse, and there were even a few detractors in his own day. His most notable contemporary critic was that great pioneer in the fight for indigenous rights, the Spanish priest Bartolomé de las Casas. To las Casas, Hernán Cortés was not a hero but a cold-blooded killer.

Ultimately, Hernán Cortés's life would be a mixture of success and adulation and scandal and despair. At one point, he was even accused of killing his wife, Catalina. Cortés and Catalina were seen in a very heated public argument. Catalina was found dead in her bed the next morning. She had bruising around her neck, and some speculated that Cortés had strangled her. Others pointed out that she had chronic heart problems and attributed the bruising to Cortés shaking her in a panicked attempt to get her heart to start beating again.

Cortés returned to Mexico in his later years and renewed his quest for exploration, traveling all the way up to what is now California. He would ultimately hang up his conquistador's hat in the 1540s, living out the rest of his days in quiet retirement in Seville, Spain. He would often reminisce about his glory days with friends and critics alike until he perished a tired old man, worn beyond his years, in 1547 at the age of sixty-two.

In Mexico today, Cortés is certainly not a popular figure. Ever since Mexico achieved independence from Spain in the 19th century, Mexicans, who have the inescapable heritage of the convergence of Spanish and indigenous cultures, have tended to view Cortés in a bad light, as nothing short of a destroyer of civilization. But how did the locals of Mexico view the intervention of Cortés and his compatriots in the immediate aftermath of the toppling of Tenochtitlan?

Though the Spanish were likely viewed as tyrants, their tyranny was seen through the contemporary lens of the constant upheaval of the day. Various groups in Mesoamerica had long been battling it out for dominance long before Cortés even arrived on the scene. In that sense, the Spaniards, as fearsome as they might have been, were likely viewed in this same context. They were simply seen as the latest group among many who had managed to gain dominance.

The lasting impact of these newcomers was likely not fully realized until later on. The Spaniards were viewed as new power players, and one could throw in their lot with them, actively resist, or pay tribute until another more dominant player came along.

As it pertains to the Tlaxcala, they chose to become allies with the Spaniards. They not only aided in the conquest of Tenochtitlan, but they also tagged along with the Spaniards in the 1524 conquest of Guatemala. The region of Central America now known as Guatemala had been inhabited for thousands of years by the Maya civilization.

The Maya reached the high point of their civilization long before the conquistadors arrived. The reasons for their decline are not exactly known, but their power had already diminished considerably by the time of the conquistadors. However, the Maya still maintained a loose network of states in the region at the time of the Spanish conquest, most notably in the Guatemalan Highlands and on the Pacific coast.

This invasion force was led by conquistador Pedro de Alvarado. Pedro was an adventurer, and he was ready to live up to the precedent that Hernán Cortés had already set. He was actually dispatched by Cortés. After toppling the Aztecs, the crafty Cortés had actually made use of Montezuma's records to figure out what surrounding territories had been paying tribute to the Aztec Empire. Polities in Guatemala were apparently on this list, so Cortés sent Alvarado, flanked by the Spaniards' Tlaxcalan allies, to investigate.

Alvarado was only around twenty-five years old at the time, but he was destined to make an impact that far outshined his relative youth and inexperience. On December 6th, 1523, his expedition began. Alvarado's forces are said to have consisted of some four hundred Spaniards, supported by as many as ten thousand indigenous auxiliaries, most of them Tlaxcalans, along with some Aztecs who decided to throw in their lot with the conquistadors.

The expedition was a costly one to finance, but Cortés figured that if enough treasure was recovered, it would be more than worth the effort. As was the case in the conquest of the Aztec Empire, the Maya of Central America had already been afflicted by the spread of smallpox before the Spaniards even arrived in the region. The invisible contagion had spread from the Caribbean to Mexico and on down into Central America. By the time the Spanish troops arrived, many Maya had died, and their potential opponents had been severely weakened by the ravages of this illness.

Even so, the Spaniards found the Maya they encountered to be entirely defiant. Upon Alvarado's arrival in Central America, he dispatched a message to the leader of a local Maya group called the K'iche (also sometimes spelled as Quiche) and issued the usual demands of submission to the Catholic Church and the Spanish Crown. The K'iche ignored the demands and instead attempted to unite various polities in the region that had previously been at odds to stand as a united front against the invaders. Ultimately, they organized thousands of warriors to take on the threat.

Demonstrating how important their religious beliefs were, immediately before engaging the Spaniards in battle, this group of warriors partook in religious festivities that included special rituals, as well as war dances. These were done in an effort to prepare themselves for the coming conflict. The ceremonies were of particular importance for K'iche commander Tecum, who was said to have been imbued with special powers that gave him the ability to see far afield and know his enemy's movements.

More likely, Tecum learned from his many spies that Alvarado and his man were approaching the highlands where he and his troops were waiting for him. The K'iche had superior numbers, but as was often the case, the Spanish guns, horses, and steel greatly minimized any numerical advantage the K'iche might have had. The Spanish infantry, along with their auxiliaries, mowed down the K'iche warriors who came their way. The K'iche were quite stunned by their heavy losses and soon made overtures for peace.

But first, they invited Alvarado to a feast supposedly being held in his honor in the K'iche town of Utatlan. Such things might sound a bit suspicious to the reader, and Alvarado himself felt the same way. Right in the middle of making his way to meet up with those holding a banquet in his honor, he suddenly changed his mind and turned back. His decision to do so likely saved his life since he avoided what would have been a deadly ambush.

Shortly thereafter, the final battle between the two sides took place. This battle resulted in the total defeat of the K'iche. Many of their leaders were killed, and the city of Utatlan was set ablaze.

This was only one piece of the Guatemalan puzzle, as there were many more polities of this political patchwork to conquer. Alvarado would take on twelve separate Maya kingdoms with varying results, but the methods were the same. He would insist they submit to the Spanish Crown, and if they refused, he dropped the hammer down on them.

Even with their guns and swords, it was an exhaustive effort to subdue all of these kingdoms. Alvarado soon came to view the results as not being all worth the effort since treasures like gold and silver were not being found in abundance.

Even worse, some of their auxiliaries from the Kaqchikel tribe suddenly turned on them. The Kaqchikels slipped away from the Spanish camp in the middle of the night, only to begin launching sporadic raids against their former allies.

Nevertheless, the Spaniards persevered and formed what would become the first Spanish outpost in Guatemala. This conquest began in 1524. The Spanish were faced with significant revolts by the locals. Because of this, the Spaniards had to found the capital—Santiago de los Caballeros—two times, with its final installment occurring in 1527. Alvarado arrived in Mexico shortly thereafter to boast of the success of his conquest.

Neighboring Honduras was subdued by Spanish conquistador Cristóbal de Olid. The conquest was initially fairly easy and straightforward—that is until Cristóbal went on a major ego trip and attempted to carve out his own independent kingdom where he could essentially be a dictator.

Hernán Cortés, who was now toeing the line for the king of Spain, was not going to let such things happen. Disobedience was all well and good when he was a renegade disobeying direct orders from the governor of Cuba, but Hernán Cortés had become the governor of a huge swathe of conquered territories in what was then called New Spain. Now, he was the one trying to maintain order in his own conquered dominion.

He left his post in Mexico City and headed to Honduras to deal with this insubordinate troublemaker himself. This meant a trek through some rather inhospitable terrain. After Cortés and his entourage became lost in the Petén rain forest, many assumed that the grand conquistador was dead.

However, Cortés eventually found his way out and made his way to Honduras. When he arrived, he learned the situation had apparently already solved itself. Cristóbal de Olid had been taken out of power and executed. Conquistador Francisco de las Casas, working under the authority of Cortés, had hunted down Cristóbal himself. However, historians are not exactly sure how Cristóbal was killed in the end.

Some accounts claim that Francisco de las Casas had him beheaded, while some other accounts claim that he was done in by his own troops, who switched sides on him at the last minute and killed him. Whatever the case may have been, Hernán Cortés was likely relieved that his little problem in Honduras had been eliminated.

Spain's Iberian cousin Portugal was also making some major inroads. While the Portuguese were busy circumnavigating the southern tip of Africa to get to India, they accidentally landed on the eastern coast of South America. Due to the abundance of brazilwood in the local forests, the Portuguese dubbed their find "Brazil."

An illustration of the discovery of Brazil.
https://commons.wikimedia.org/wiki/File:Pedro-e-297-a_0001_1_p24-C-R01.50_cropped.jpg

Although Brazil was first discovered in 1500, it took some time for the Portuguese to get serious about establishing lasting colonies there. It was not until 1534 that the Portuguese monarch, King John III, established an official charter for the creation of captaincies on the South American mainland. These captaincies were organized settlements that focused on sugar production.

Brazil's climate was quite good for growing sugar. So, even though there was no gold in "them thar hills," there was ample sunshine to grow sugar in the fields.

Sugar plantations are labor intensive, so it was not long before the Portuguese began impressing the locals into service. Ever since the days of Christopher Columbus, European explorers did not hesitate to engage the natives in forced labor if it suited their purpose.

The indigenous people used for this enterprise were the Tupi, a seminomadic group who lived near the coast. The Tupi were friendly and did not pose any threat to the Portuguese, but that did not stop Portuguese settlers from attempting to exploit them. The only thing that put an end to this labor pool was Tupis fleeing in droves and perishing from imported diseases from Europe.

When the Portuguese could not find enough workers for their fields, they began to turn to Africa for slaves. The Portuguese had already developed close ties with several outposts along the African coast during their forays circumnavigating the tip of Africa. Through these points of reference and contact, they would begin importing human cargo from the African continent to the Americas.

It is an awful truth, but this imported slave labor allowed major Portuguese settlements, such as Bahia, Pernambuco, and, of course, Rio de Janeiro, to be built up and prosper. And as these settlements grew, more and more immigrants from Portugal arrived. Portugal, a European country only a fraction of the size of Spain, was fairly overcrowded at the time, so the incentive to migrate was considerable.

The Portuguese became creative. Along with willing immigrants, they also forced prisoners to go to the colony to work as a means of restitution. These folks were dubbed degredados. Even though they were toward the bottom of the social strata in the colony, they held out hope that they might one day be able to lead a better life.

The owners of all of those sugar plantations became the super-rich of Brazil. The nascent Brazilians were doing well enough for themselves, but the sugar business was a gradual one and would take some time to grow.

The Spaniards were far more interested in finding great wealth already in existence that they could plunder instead of building up wealth.

They would be in luck. Shortly after Mexico and much of Central America had been thoroughly plundered and pacified, reports came in of another great indigenous civilization to despoil located thousands of miles to the southwest in a land that would come to be called Peru.

Chapter 5 – The Plundering of Peru

"Here there are only two guilty parties: You for subjugating my people and me for wanting to free them."

-Tupac Amaru II

 The actual name given to Peru by its indigenous inhabitants has been lost in the sands of history. The current designation of Peru is believed to stem from a misunderstanding between a Spaniard and a local. A Spaniard had asked a local a simple question: "What land is this?" The local, who only knew a smattering of Spanish, apparently misunderstood the question. The local man thought that the Spaniard was asking him who he was. The man's name was Biru, but when he uttered the name, the Spaniard heard Peru.

 This story cannot be verified, but if this did happen, then Peru's name came about as one misunderstanding piled on top of another misunderstanding. And the fact that this land would come to be ravaged and despoiled as much as it was, its rightful name being defaced seems almost fitting.

 When the first Spaniards arrived on the scene, they found that the land of Peru was recovering from turmoil. The scourge of smallpox that had been spreading like wildfire all across the Americas had finally reached Peru.

 Like the rest of their Native American brethren, the Peruvians had no natural defense against this Old World disease. Unlike the European explorers, who had built up immunities from centuries of dealing with this sickness, the natives of the New World were especially vulnerable to these outbreaks. By the 1520s, the contagion had reached the courts of the Inca royals. In 1527, the Inca ruler Huayna Capac perished from the disease. His death was followed by the death of his son Ninan Cuyochi, who was next in line for the throne.

According to Inca legend, the great Huayna Capac, just prior to his death, actually made a prediction that his empire would soon come to an end at the hands of outsiders. It is hard to know if this deathbed prediction actually occurred as described or if it was embellished after the fact. It could also be that Huayna Capac's feverish mind had a hard time thinking of anything other than apocalyptic destruction.

But whatever the case might have been, the Inca Empire truly was on the brink of destruction. Immediately after Huayna Capac's and Ninan Cuyochi's deaths, the Inca world was torn asunder as two surviving sons of Huayna Capac—Huáscar and Atahualpa—duked it out for supremacy. The Inca civilization descended into the chaos of civil war. Eventually, Huáscar was defeated, and his brother, Atahualpa, was able to proclaim himself the sole ruler of the realm.

But soon after he put his brother and former challenger away, news reached Atahualpa's ears of strange foreigners who had been encountered trespassing on the land he had fought so hard to secure. In 1531, conquistador Francisco Pizarro and his ragtag group of explorers set up shop on the shores of Peru. They had landed in their sailing vessels, which to the locals seemed like floating mountains of wood.

It was also reported that these men had strong, steel swords, and the Spaniards' guns elicited tales of men wielding the power of lightning in their hands. Even more shocking to the locals was the sight of the Spaniards' horses. The people of Peru had never seen a horse before, and to them, these giant steeds seemed like some sort of mythical monster.

All of these whispered rumors about strangers led to many questions. Who were they? What were they? Many did not even think they were normal men at all. The Peruvians had never witnessed anything quite so strange; encountering these strangers was far different from what they normally encountered.

However, the Inca ruler, Atahualpa, was not going to be so easily spooked, and thanks to his robust intelligence network on the ground, he figured out these visitors were ordinary men. They might have strange beasts, big ships, and mighty weapons, but they were men all the same.

His spies reported back that there was nothing supernatural about these visitors. They reported that the men ate, used the bathroom, and even cavorted with local women, just as any other human being might.

In fact, the spies suggested the only thing special about these newcomers was their disrespect for common decency. Considering as much, the Inca emperor's advisors urged him to take action and drive off the intruders before it was too late. But even so, Atahualpa remained ambivalent about the whole thing. He was not quite sure how to respond to the intrusion.

In the meantime, Francisco Pizzaro was making progress as he traveled through Atahualpa's realm. He managed to dispatch a trusted associate, Captain Hernando de Soto—to see what he could find out. Hernando wanted to gain access to the Inca emperor, which he achieved. But if Hernando de Soto thought that he could sweet talk the Inca ruler into granting concessions to the Spaniards, he had another thing coming.

Although the Inca ruler approached the strangers in a peaceful fashion, after initial greetings were exchanged, he proceeded to give Hernando a severe tongue-lashing. He accused Hernando de Soto and his compatriots of violating his land and mistreating his subjects. Atahualpa had apparently heard reports that Spaniards had roughed up some locals, and he was ready to let these interlopers know that he was none too pleased with what had happened.

Hernando de Soto, for his part, realized that he was in a precarious position and was pragmatic enough to take the abuse. If he were to do anything to make the Inca emperor upset, he knew that with a mere gesture, he could order his guards to seize him. And despite their guns and swords, de Soto and the few Spaniards who accompanied him hardly would have been able to have withstood hundreds of angry Inca warriors leaping upon them all at once.

As such, Hernando de Soto wisely kept his cool. He even apologized to placate the Inca ruler's wrath, insisting that the reports were exaggerated. Atahualpa apparently accepted the apology and let de Soto go. However, considering what happened next, it would have been in Atahualpa's best interest if he had seized de Soto and then mobilized for an all-out war against Pizzaro and his men.

But that was not what happened. Atahualpa took de Soto up on an invitation to meet his boss Pizzaro and the rest of the conquistadors at the village of Cajamarca in November 1532. When the Inca king arrived in the town square of Cajamarca that November, he found it strangely deserted. It did not take long for his spies to get back to him as to the whereabouts of the Spaniards.

It was reported that the Spanish were hiding inside several buildings around the town square. But even though the Inca emperor's intelligence gathering was accurate, the interpretation as to why the Spaniards were hiding was hopelessly flawed. It was assumed the Spaniards were hiding out of fear and timidity. This was partially correct. Many of the Spaniards were indeed afraid. The spies had borne witness to the fear etched on the men's faces and how they could barely keep their shaking knees from knocking together as they stood in place.

Many of his troops were understandably terrified at the notion that a handful of Spaniards would somehow take on thousands of Inca warriors. Nevertheless, their prospects were bleak. What else could they do? Toss their weapons to the side and run off into the wilderness? If they abandoned Pizzaro now, they would most likely perish in Peru. So, even though they were terrified of what Pizzaro was getting them into, they likely felt as if they had no choice but to comply.

So yes, the Inca emperor's spies were correct in their reports that the Spaniards were hiding and that many of them seemed scared. But the fatal flaw in these intelligence reports was the main reason why the men were hiding. The Spaniards' obvious ambush was misinterpreted and perceived as the Spaniards suddenly turning into a bunch of cowards and hiding themselves at the last minute.

This flawed estimation of events had Atahualpa lead his men right into the center of this trap. Atahualpa urged the hidden Spaniards to come forth. But the only ones to come out were a priest, Father Vicente de Valverde, and his translator. Speaking through his translator, the priest began to needle Atahualpa about his religious beliefs. This likely caught the Inca emperor off-guard, as he expected to speak with the strangers about more practical matters, not engage in a theological debate.

But the Spaniards, no matter how devious some of their ulterior motives might have been, kept to a familiar script. Any time they encountered a new civilization, they made sure to "read them their rights." Like a beat cop telling folks they have the right to remain silent just before slapping on the cuffs, the Spaniards had to rattle off the Requerimiento.

Atahualpa was told that he was required to pay respects to King Charles of Spain and the pope of the Roman Catholic Church and to embrace Christianity. One can only imagine how confused Emperor Atahualpa must have been.

However, it was apparently when the priest referenced his Bible as a book that contained the Word of God that the priest really got the Inca ruler's attention. It is worth noting that the Incas did not use books. Instead, they stored information by way of quipu, which was basically a system of knotted cords that allowed them to keep records. Some think that perhaps since the Incas were not familiar with books and did not have a term for it that the translator might have referred to the Bible as a quipu. If so, this would explain why Atahualpa might have been intrigued and then confused. When he was handed the priest's Bible, he very well might have been expecting to see the knotted quipu. The Incas understood quipus contained important information for record-keeping, and this one apparently had records directly from God.

The confused Inca king flipped through the Bible, puzzled at what he held in his hands. He clearly realized that it was not a quipu. He likely did not see the point of it and tossed the Bible on the ground.

It is believed the priest and Pizarro had assumed this would happen. If the Inca emperor rejected the Spanish Crown and Christianity, the Spanish had their reason to attack and subdue the pagans. Once the Bible hit the ground, the priest began shouting to his comrades who were hiding out in the nearby buildings. This was the signal to launch the ambush.

Suddenly, the Spaniards' guns opened up, and the startled Incas were being hit on all sides. In the midst of this chaos, Pizzaro led a cavalry charge with the full intention of rushing up to Atahualpa himself and taking him prisoner. The cunning Pizzaro knew all about what had happened to the Aztecs after Hernán Cortés captured their leader Montezuma and made him a prisoner, and he was attempting to use the same exact play against the Incas.

Pizarro knew that the Incas, like the Aztecs, had a society in which all orders had to come from the man on top—the emperor. So, if the emperor was made their prisoner, the whole Inca Empire would be theirs to control.

Unfortunately for the Incas, after an intense struggle, the Spaniards were able to break through to the startled Atahualpa and seize him. Spanish artillery hammered away at the Inca warriors until they panicked and fled.

The Spaniards took the Inca emperor back to their camp and began to interrogate him. Atahualpa was soon made aware that, along with religious concerns, these strangers had a strong interest in gold and silver. Speaking through an interpreter, he informed his hosts that he could get them plenty of these precious metals and begged for his release.

Of course, the Spaniards were not going to simply set Atahualpa free on a pledge that he would bring them gold. They were much too shrewd for that. They knew the second they let him go, the whole Inca nation would descend on top of them. Atahualpa was their human shield, and no matter what they might have told him about his eventual release, they were not about to let him go. They did, however, allow him to speak to his subordinates, and a series of relay runners allowed him to communicate the demands of the Spaniards.

Soon, thanks to the orders that Atahualpa issued while in captivity, all manner of priceless gold and silver artifacts were being brought into the Spaniards' camp. Unfortunately for Atahualpa, he would learn that the more treasures the conquistadors were given, the more they wanted.

The Spaniards were likely so focused on acquiring wealth that they did not realize that Atahualpa was issuing other orders. Along with issuing demands for silver and gold from his captivity, Atahualpa ordered the execution of his brother Huáscar, who was being held prisoner in the Inca capital of Cuzco (also spelled as Cusco).

It seems that Atahualpa was concerned that his living rival might manage to somehow depose him while he was being held hostage. Atahualpa was showing his own greed for power by carrying out this punitive act. If Atahualpa could have put his own personal desire for power aside and considered the greater good of his kingdom, he might have ordered his brother Huáscar to be freed so he could rally the troops to defend the realm. Instead, the Inca leader seemed to care only about his own grip on power.

The Spaniards were always looking for a pretext to justify their actions, and they would later use the fact that Atahualpa had engaged in this cold-blooded killing as part of their justification for his execution.

However, prior to all of this, Pizzaro came to be on quite friendly terms with the imprisoned monarch. It has been said that he even taught Atahualpa how to play chess—a game that he very much enjoyed. It probably only reinforced the mental chess match that he was frequently engaged in with his captors. Atahualpa could often only wonder what his captors were really up to. He saw plenty of gold and silver go into the camp and witnessed it all melted down into standard Spanish bars. These bars were then loaded off to be sent to waiting ships. What were they doing? Where were they taking all of this treasure? He could only wonder.

Atahualpa was in for some trouble when Pizzaro was tipped off that a large group of Incas were on their way to free the ruler. A panicked Pizzaro questioned Atahualpa about all of this, but the Inca ruler claimed to know nothing about it. Nevertheless, the Spaniards decided to put Atahualpa on trial for "treason."

It seems absurd that a man who was taken hostage would be tried for treason on the grounds that his own people might be attempting to rescue him. However, according to the warped logic of the Spaniards, the Incas were under the jurisdiction of the Spanish Crown, and any attempt to thwart their efforts was "treasonous."

Along with the treason charge, Atahualpa also faced charges of fratricide due to Huáscar's death. A shocked Atahualpa, who could not understand what was happening to him, was soon led to a stake. It is not so much that he could not understand the words rendered by the translators present but rather that he could not come to grips with the fact that the Spaniards would so easily do away with him. He had been cooperative enough so far, and now he was going to be burned alive for his cooperation?

The Spanish informed him that if he did not convert to Christianity, he would be burned alive. If he converted, he would have the small mercy of being strangled to death rather than being burned. The Incas believed the soul would not go on to the afterlife if the body was burned, so Atahualpa was baptized. He was then strangled with a garrote.

Ironically, shortly after his death, reports reached Pizzaro's ears that all of that talk of an Inca army was made up. It was just a wild rumor that had gotten out of control with no basis in reality. Francisco Pizzaro displayed one of his rare instances of remorse as this conquistador realized that he had basically put the Inca ruler to death for no reason at all.

Of course, we have to remember that most of the accounts about the natives come from Spanish journals or other eyewitness accounts. While some sources say that Pizarro cried when the Inca emperor was put to death, others do not mention it. Some accounts also mention a full trial; it seems unlikely that would have happened.

Chapter 6 – The End of the Inca Empire

"Reflect on how long my grandparents and great grandparents and I myself have looked after you, protected you, cared for you and governed—making provision that you had plenty—so do not forget us, not in your lifetimes, not in the time of your descendants. Outwardly you can give the impression of complying with their demands. Give them small tribute, whatever you can spare from your lands—for these people are so savage and so different from us that if you don't, they will take it from you by force. I know that some day, by force or deceit, they will make you worship what they worship. When that time comes, when you can no longer resist, do it in front of them, but on the other hand do not forget our ceremonies. And if they tell you to break your shrines and force you to do so, reveal only what you have to and keep the rest hidden, close to your hearts."

-*Manco Inca*

After the death of their former puppet, Atahualpa, the Spaniards knew that it would not be long before a large Inca force would be rallied by whoever turned out to be his successor. In order to maintain some sense of an advantage, Pizzaro decided to go on the offensive and take the fight to his opponents before they could effectively organize against him.

Pizarro's camp had been bolstered by hundreds of new arrivals of Spanish explorers. Even though the Spanish were still outnumbered, it was hoped that Spanish technology would help even the odds. As such, the conquistadors fastened on their swords, grabbed their guns, hopped on their horses, and charged straight for the Inca metropolis of Cuzco.

They arrived at the Inca capital on November 14th, 1533. At this point, an Inca general called Quizquiz was issuing orders and acting as the authority over the Inca armed forces. As mentioned, this small contingent of Spanish troops was dwarfed by the massive size of the Inca army, but Pizarro was depending on Spanish swords, guns, horses, and armor to save the day.

It was the latter that made the Spaniards so difficult for the Incas to inflict harm upon. The Incas fought with bronze-tipped maces. But whenever they clubbed the Spaniards over the heads with these traditional weapons, the Spaniards' armored helmets reduced the severity of the blow. To be sure, many of the Spaniards likely got a bad headache that day, but the blows were not fatal or as injurious as they would have been against an unarmored foe.

The fact that the Spaniards were on horseback also made it very difficult for the Incas to target them. Hitting someone over the head with a club is hard enough at ground level, let alone when someone is towering over you on a horse. Inca arrows and stones mostly bounced off Spanish armor and had very little effect. The Spanish, however, were quite effective, as their steel swords sliced through the Incas.

The two sides briefly halted their fighting at nightfall, and Quizquiz, realizing that his strategy was not working, made the fateful decision to abandon the city and retreat. By morning, he was gone, and the Spaniards were able to waltz right into Cuzco uncontested.

Interestingly enough, the citizens were somewhat relieved. It is not that they were happy to see the Spaniards so much that they were happy to see Quizquiz and his army depart. Quizquiz and his troops were essentially an occupying army and had been dominating Cuzco ever since Atahualpa had defeated his brother Huáscar. Cuzco was full of Huáscar supporters, so many Incas were not friendly to Atahualpa, Quizquiz, or his army.

Pizarro soon became aware of these sentiments and sought to exploit them as much as possible. He even managed to locate another brother of Atahualpa, Manco Inca Yupanqui, and install him as the new Inca emperor. But, of course, the Spaniards intended him to be yet another useful puppet ruler. And the first order Manco Inca Yupanqui was given from his Spanish benefactors was to cobble together an army of Inca warriors and dispatch them to take out Quizquiz and his followers.

This army was able to track down Quizquiz, and skirmishes ensued, but Quizquiz remained one step ahead. It was not until his own demoralized troops rebelled against him that his end would come. He was ultimately killed by one of his own soldiers who refused to continue marching to his orders.

In the meantime, Manco Inca Yupanqui was officially coronated, and in a surprising show of support, Manco accepted the Requerimiento. It remains unclear if the Incas who had heard what was happening understood, but Peru would most certainly never be the same again.

Manco was left to rule Cuzco as the Spaniards built up their base on the Peruvian coast, establishing a settlement they called Lima in 1535. Lima was also the hub where all of those recently melted down gold and silver treasures of the Incas were being shipped as gold bars to Spain.

In order to understand the bigger geopolitical picture of what was transpiring at this time, let us take a look at what was occurring in Europe. In 1535, the Holy Roman Empire, backed by the Catholic Church, found itself locked in an epic struggle with the Islamic powerhouse of the Ottoman Turks. The resurgent Turks had shocked the world by conquering one of the former capitals of Christendom—Constantinople—in 1453. The Ottoman war machine continued to advance and managed to reach the very gates of Vienna, Austria, by 1529.

The Turks were also conducting heavy raids across the Mediterranean by the 1530s and even launching attacks on Italy. The Ottoman Empire stretched through the Balkans, the Middle East, and all of North Africa and was threatening to encircle the entire Mediterranean world. Charles V was able to counteract the Turkish advance by seizing Tunis off the North African coast in 1535, which proved decisive in diverting Turkish forces away from more vulnerable targets.

It has been said that all of these wars waged by the forces of the Holy Roman Empire and the Catholic Church were largely funded by the gold and silver flowing from Peru. As terrible as the actions perpetuated by Francisco Pizzaro might seem, world history certainly could have taken a very different turn if this readily available source of revenue had not been available.

At any rate, even though Manco Inca Yupanqui was superficially in charge of Cuzco, Pizzaro had placed fellow conquistador Diego de Almagro as an administrator. Manco ultimately had to report to him. Almagro and Manco seemed to get along well enough, but after Almagro left for a planned expedition farther south that July, all hell would break loose.

Almagro would place Juan and Gonzalo Pizzaro in charge while he was away, leading an expedition into what would become modern Chile. Juan and Gonzalo were Francisco Pizzaro's younger brothers. The two men were not only untested in leadership roles, but they were also, by all accounts, exceedingly crass, cruel, and troublemaking blowhards. Such descriptions may sound unnecessarily harsh, but in consideration of their actions, most would find them rather accurate.

These guys basically lorded over Cuzco, taking whatever they wanted from the populace. They seized treasure and, even more distressing, seized people if it suited their fancy. Most distressing of all was Juan Pizzaro's attempts to bed Manco's own wife. Needless to say, Manco finally had enough of these antics, and in November 1535, he began what would become a long and bitter revolt against the Spanish conquest of Peru.

The Spaniards thought they had Manco Inca Yupanqui under their control, but all Manco had to do was speak the words, and he was able to ignite a rebellion throughout Peru. As soon as the Spaniards figured out what was afoot, they tossed Manco into a jail cell. Pizzaro's brother Hernando arrived on the scene, fresh from Spain, in January of 1536 and was infuriated to learn of his brothers', Juan and Gonzalo's antics.

Hernando Pizzaro was sensible enough to admit that Manco had every right to be upset. He also had direct instructions from Charles V that Manco should be treated well and rewarded for his cooperation with the Crown. After all, hadn't Manco accepted the Requerimiento? Hernando immediately set Manco loose and put him back on the throne.

Manco, for his part, acted as if all was forgiven and that everything would soon turn back to normal. However, it would soon be learned that Manco had a great poker face. After what he had been through, he was determined to exact his vengeance on the Spaniards. Still feigning cooperation, on April 18th, 1536, Manco Inco Yupanqui requested permission (yes, even though he was king, he had to clear everything with the Spaniards) to head to a holy Inca shrine.

Hernando Pizzaro was apparently still deeply remorseful over what had occurred, as he obliged this wish without hesitation. This would prove to be a major mistake. As soon as Manco Inco Yupanqui was out of sight, he disappeared. Shortly thereafter, a large army of Incas besieged the Spaniards at Cuzco. The Spaniards sought to charge out of the trap they had found themselves in several times but were mercilessly hammered with stones, arrows, and clubs.

Even so, the causalities were always much higher on the Inca side than on the Spanish side during these exchanges. Even after Manco Inca Yupanqui set fire to his own former capital city, the Spaniards persevered. Facing mounting casualties, the Incas pulled back to the Inca fortress of Sacsayhuamán, where they once again engaged the Spaniards in a series of terrific and bloody battles. During these exchanges, Juan Pizzaro—the chief mischief maker himself—would perish after he was hit in the head with a large stone.

At the same time all of this was going on, one of Manco's generals, a man whose name comes down to us as Quizo Yupanqui, was simultaneously leading an assault on the forces of Francisco Pizzaro based out of Lima. The forces of Quizo staged several ambushes on the road leading out of Lima in 1536, in which he was able to kill hundreds of Spaniards who were sent out as reinforcements. These feats were achieved by Quizo's men taking the high ground and simply waiting for the Spaniards to pass through narrow passages so that they could bombard them with boulders from above. Quizo's assaults leveled the playing field by utilizing the advantage of Peru's natural terrain. However, as successful as Quizo's exploits were, they would not amount to much.

By 1537, Manco was holed up in an Inca fortress called Ollantaytambo. His troops were confronted by a group of resurgent Spaniards led by Hernando de Soto. Manco Inca Yupanqui surprised his foes by having his men redirect surrounding canals so that water suddenly came flooding through the plains.

The Spaniards, with their horses nearly up to their necks in water, were unable to effectively maneuver. Soon, Inca warriors were charging forward and pummeling them with stones and arrows. The Spaniards had no choice but to flee. They were chased all the way back to Cuzco. If it were not for Spanish armor and the relative inability of Inca weaponry to penetrate that armor, the Spaniards likely would have been completely annihilated.

Quizo, in the meantime, had received new marching orders from Manco to storm into Lima and take Francisco Pizzaro prisoner. Quizo, who had been so successful in the field by carefully ambushing the Spaniards on high, likely knew that these orders were foolish, but he had no choice but to follow them. He sent his troops on charge after suicidal charge, only for him and all of his men to be butchered by Spanish swords and guns.

The situation was about to get even more complex when Diego de Almagro suddenly returned from an expedition in Chile and expressed his frustration with how Manco had been treated. Almagro, a rough-hewed and entirely duplicitous figure, seemed to sense an opportunity to increase his own stature.

He was shrewd enough to dress up his ambition as a bid to right the wrongs of the past, but by all accounts, Diego de Almagro was a pure and simple opportunist who was seeking to seize power by any means possible. And in this instance, he attempted to do so by presenting himself to Manco as an ally so that he and Manco's Inca forces could defeat the Pizzaro family. Manco balked at the offer, apparently not willing to align himself any further with the Spaniards who had betrayed his trust.

Nevertheless, with or without Manco, Almagro meant business and launched a coup to seize control of Cuzco. While the two factions of conquistadors were battling it out, Manco took what remained of his army and traveled to a remote refuge in the farthest corners of the Inca territory. From here, the Incas would continue to rule a rump Inca state until 1572, when the last Inca ruler and the last vestige of the Inca state finally came to an end.

Chapter 7 – The Conquest of the Rest of South America

"As soon as I arrived in the Indies, in the first island which I found, I took some of the natives by force, in order that they might learn and might give me information of whatever there is in these parts. And so it was that they soon understood us and we them. Either by speech or by signs, and they have been very serviceable."

-Christopher Columbus

Further conquest of other regions would be carried out of out of Spanish-occupied Peru, which at that time still contained Bolivia. It was Peru, in particular, that the conquistadors first pushed out of and into neighboring Chile.

Chile was a harsh, remote environment, and its terrain proved to be quite a challenge. Peru boasted some of the fiercest fighters on the continent, a tribe known as the Araucanians. Even though the Spaniards had Spanish steel and horses, the Araucanians were such fearless, audacious fighters that they often got the better of the Spaniards in these early engagements.

Interestingly, the Araucanians of Chile had long fought off attempts by the Incas to annex their territory, thereby terminating the Incas' expansion into what we now know as Bolivia. Once the Spaniards superseded the Incas, the Araucanians carried out the same resistance that had long thwarted the Incas against the Spanish.

Conquistador Diego de Almagro was the first Spaniard to cross the Atacama Desert and encounter these warriors. This epic encounter occurred in 1536. Almagro and his entourage barely escaped with their lives. His failure to make a name for himself in Chile explains why he returned to Peru determined to oust the Pizzaro family so that he could try to stake a larger claim in Peru.

Almagro's revolt ultimately failed, and he would perish in a Peruvian jail cell in 1538. All the same, before he perished, his tales of what lay in Chile would inspire others to make further attempts to travel to this new frontier. Explorer Pedro de Valdivia would lead a renewed push into Chilean territory in 1540. This fresh batch of explorers was successful in setting up a permanent settlement, which was situated near the Mapocho River.

The following year, 1541, saw the small settlement assaulted by an indigenous tribe. Valdivia was not at the settlement at the time, and Valdivia's mistress, Inés Suárez, held down the fort and led the defense of this colonial outpost. The settlers survived the ordeal, and in gratitude of the fact that they would live to see another day, they named the settlement Santiago de Nueva Extremadura—a title that would later become simply Santiago.

The original name was in partial reference to the town of Extremadura, Spain. Nueva means "new," and Santiago is a patron saint. Put it together, and you basically have Santiago of New Extremadura. This settlement would eventually become Chile's capital—Santiago de Chile—and it would continue to grow until it was one of the most robust cities in the Americas.

Valdivia led further expeditions, pushing farther south and skirmishing with the dreaded Araucanian warriors along the way. In 1553, Valdivia led an expedition that had a particularly violent outcome, in which he and most of his men lost their lives.

Prior to being killed, Valdivia had actually been taken prisoner. He died shortly thereafter, although the exact nature of his death is disputed. Some accounts claim that he was beheaded. Another more riveting (not to mention gruesome) account states that his forearms were chopped off, cooked, and eaten by his enemies.

Depiction of Spanish treatment toward the natives. On the right-hand side, you can see the natives engaging in cannibalism.

https://commons.wikimedia.org/wiki/File:Narratio_Regionum_indicarum_per_Hispanos_Quosdam_devastatarum_verissima_Theodore_de_Bry.jpg

After Valdivia's death, the governor of Peru sent his son, Don García Hurtado de Mendoza, to become the governor of Chile. It would become Mendoza's primary task to neutralize the menace that the Araucanian tribe posed to the Spanish conquest. He was successful in his efforts, and in 1558, he managed to take the leader of the Araucanians, Caupolicán, prisoner. He had Caupolicán publicly executed in the Chilean town of Cañete to serve as an example and a warning to others.

Spanish conquistadors first managed to cross the Chilean section of the Andes and stumble into the land that is now called Argentina in the year 1536. The first settlement, which was established on the future site of Buenos Aires, was abandoned in 1541. Further attempts to settle Argentina would not be made until the 1580s.

Just to the east of Argentina, Spanish explorers blazed a path into what would become Paraguay. Here, they founded the city of Asunción in 1537. It was named in recognition of the Catholic holiday celebrating

Mother Mary called the Assumption of the Virgin Mary.

The settlers made a man named Domingo Martínez de Irala their governor, but he was not officially backed by the Spanish Crown. This land was inhabited largely by the Guarani tribe, which had settled in the region for a thousand years. Domingo displayed a surprising (or at least surprising for most conquistadors) degree of tolerance and had good relations with the local Guarani.

Domingo Martínez de Irala supposedly married several daughters of a local Guarani chief in clear defiance of Catholic prohibitions against polygamous marriage. Not only that, but he also made sure to respect Guarani culture and took pride in the fact that he was considered a part of the Guarani fabric.

Nevertheless, the Spanish Crown did not approve of Domingo's rule and sent a statesman and former conquistador by the name of Cabeza de Vaca to take over.

Cabeza de Vaca is an interesting character. He had been on his own adventures of conquest in the Americas before briefly returning to Spain. In fact, Cabeza de Vaca was one of the first to push into the far northern frontiers of Mexico.

At any rate, Cabeza de Vaca showed up in March 1542 and almost immediately rubbed the settlers the wrong way. He arrived on the scene, trying to tell everyone what to do and how to live their lives. Most distressing to the settlers, he began making plans to transfer the settlement farther down the Paraguay River to the so-called "Mouth of the Plata."

This was distressing because prior to Cabeza de Vaca's arrival, this location had already been attempted, and it had proved fruitless. No one likes to repeat the same mistake twice, yet here was someone, fresh from Spain, ordering them to do something they knew would only result in failure. The settlers balked at the notion, and the disagreement was so fierce that Cabeza de Vaca lost his nerve and backed off on the idea.

Nevertheless, he quickly convened his own court, established tax collection, and began to try and enforce his will on the community. This included the enforcement of Catholic norms as it pertained to traditional marriage. This caused much consternation. The Paraguayan settlers were accustomed to the polygamous arrangements that often took place and did not like the idea of going back to having only.

Again, Governor Cabeza de Vaca found he had another thing coming. The Paraguayan settlers were not going to give up their wives for this crony of the Spanish Crown. Besides any sentimental attachment, the polygamous unions had served a major role in the interconnected nature of the community. The settlers were connected to the Guarani tribe through these multiple unions, and the family connections they had forged were too important for the settlers to turn their back on them.

Instead, the settlers turned on the governor and threw him in a jail cell. They then took the incredible step of building Cabeza de Vaca a ship to send him back to Spain! After Cabeza de Vaca's altogether embarrassing return to Spain in 1545, the Spanish Crown apparently knew not to push the Paraguayans too far and relented in its demands.

This enabled the Paraguayans to reinstate their old handpicked governor Irala. He would remain the governor until he died in 1556.

Jesuit priests would set up shop in Paraguay in 1588 and began working vigorously with the Guarani. They taught them about Christianity, farming, textiles, and other important trades. They did this to make the Guarani more self-sufficient so they could better avoid being preyed upon by Spanish administrators. Pretty soon, the region had become a kind of "safe zone" for the Guarini, who were also allowed to keep many of their traditions intact. This safe haven would last until King Charles III of Spain decided to dismantle it in 1767.

More land was waiting to be ventured into farther south of Paraguay. This region would ultimately become yet another South American nation—Uruguay. The nation of Uruguay as we know it today was largely settled in the 1680s by the Spaniards' Iberian cousins, the Portuguese. However, Spanish explorers would come to contest Portuguese dominance and would later seize much of the territory for themselves.

The main holdings of the Portuguese would continue to be Brazil despite the fact that the major Uruguayan city of Colonia do Sacramento was founded by them. The Portuguese also founded Guanare in the Central American region now known as Venezuela.

Venezuela got its name as far back as 1499, when the esteemed explorer Amerigo Vespucci, admiring the stilt houses of the indigenous people, stated that it reminded him of "Veneziola" or "Little Venice." The region would go through many fits and starts until it was officially incorporated into the Viceroyalty of New Granada in 1717, which made it part of a large chunk of South America that would eventually be divvied up into the modern-day nations of Colombia, Ecuador, Panama, and Venezuela.

Chapter 8 – The Conquest of Southwestern North America

"One third of our people were dangerously ill, getting worse hourly, and we felt sure of meeting the same fate, with death as our only prospect, which in such a country was much worse yet."

-Cabeza de Vaca

The push into northern Mexico received a boost when Cabeza de Vaca led a small party into the Sonora Valley in 1536. Here, they met some friendly indigenous people who treated them to a dinner of dressed deer hearts. These conquistadors, who had no doubt heard of the stories of Aztecs and Maya ripping out the hearts of human sacrificial victims, were probably just glad the menu consisted of deer hearts rather than human ones!

Not all of Cabeza de Vaca's reports were positive, however. He also reported that there were fierce archers in the land who used poison-tipped arrows capable of striking anyone dead.

At any rate, this was one of the first forays farther afield as it pertained to Spanish holdings in Mexico. From roughly 1540 to 1609, Spanish explorers embarked upon a major push to capitalize on some of what Cabeza de Vaca had discovered.

The campaign to push out of the frontier of northern Mexico began, and the Spanish would make their way into what would later become the southwestern states of the future United States of America. The territories the Spanish discovered would run from California in the west through the modern-day states of Nevada, Arizona, New Mexico, Texas, and all the way to Florida.

Hernando de Soto was another conquistador who played a major role in these early forays. He was the one who had led the charge to Florida and then on to what would become Georgia, Alabama, Mississippi, and perhaps even as far afield as Arkansas.

De Soto had heard accounts of Cabeza de Vaca's wanderings, and he wanted to learn more. He led a group of hundreds of explorers. They set sail from Havana, Cuba, and headed north to Florida. Although it is still disputed, it is widely believed that de Soto's expedition landed in what is now Manatee County, Florida, on the southern edge of Tampa Bay.

Here, he and his group fought their way through the Florida Panhandle and then headed northwest to Georgia, Alabama, and Mississippi. To say they fought their way through Florida is not really an exaggeration since they encountered an extremely hostile tribe, the Timucua, whose warriors seemed intent on ambushing the visitors just about every step of their trek through Florida.

It is said that along with these intermittent skirmishes, two major all-out battles were fought, one of which resulted in the massacre of Timucua warriors. De Soto also came into contact with the Apalachee tribe when he camped at the site of Anhaica (modern-day Tallahassee) up in the northern Florida Panhandle.

De Soto's group then headed in a northeasterly direction into what is now Georgia. They supposedly traveled in this direction when they were informed by locals that they could find gold "toward the sun's rising." The archaeological record proves that de Soto traveled along this path, as artifacts left by the Spaniards dating back to this period have been found.

However, the Spaniards did not find any gold in the Georgian hills, so they continued traveling northeast until they hit the Carolinas. They then went west to Tennessee before heading back south to Alabama.

Conquistador Francisco Vázquez de Coronado is another towering figure who looms large in the early explorations of the southern United States. Dubbed the "Knight of Pueblos and Plains," the epic Coronado expedition launched in February 1540 and would expand much further on previous explorations. This expedition had Coronado leading some four hundred Spaniards and over a thousand indigenous allies across what would later become the southwestern United States. From the sheer numbers he brought with him, it seems clear that he was prepared for hostilities should they arise.

During this journey, he traversed up the coast of Baja California, keeping the Gulf of California on his western flank. He reached the northernmost Mexican settlement at the time, San Miguel de Culiacán, on March 28th, 1540. Here, they rested for a bit before moving northward up the inland trail.

As they progressed, supplies for such a large contingent of people began to become a concern. It was noted that water and grazing grounds for animals were limited on this trail, so Coronado decided to split up his group into several smaller units. These smaller groups would travel at varying intervals up the main trail so that the available resources would not become prematurely exhausted. The fact that Coronado would plan ahead like this demonstrates pragmatic decisiveness on his part.

The explorers traveled up the coast in this piecemeal fashion, making their way to the Sinaloa River, which they followed north through the mountains before reaching the Yaqui River. They followed the Río Sonora to the Huachuca Mountains before crossing a stream, passing through a river valley, and traveling through a wilderness terrain that took them to what is now southern Arizona.

It was here that the Spaniards first encountered the Pueblo people, later named after the architectural style of their pueblo structures. The first Pueblo group encountered by Coronado's expedition was the Zuni.

Members of Coronado's expedition managed to reach what would later be dubbed the Colorado River.

These were the first forays. But interestingly enough, the real incentive for the Spanish explorers that truly got the ball rolling was reports in 1579 that English privateer Francis Drake had found the fabled Northwest Passage that would allow ships to seamlessly sail to East Asia via a western route, allowing easy trade with China and India. Drake had not found the passage (it would not be discovered until 1854, and it would not be traversed fully by sea until after the 20th century began), but this rumor piqued the curiosity of many.

The idea of a Northwest Passage caused an explosion of explorations. The Spaniards did not want to be outdone by any European competitors. In a similar vein as the Space Race, which had the Americans and the Russians seeking to be the first to get to the moon, the Spaniards wanted to be the first to find the Northwest Passage.

During this push, in the 1580s, the Spaniards mapped out the lands of the Pueblo people. The territory of the Pueblo Indians would ultimately be annexed by the Spaniards and turned into New Mexico in the year 1598. This was a vast territory that would include not just the modern-day state of New Mexico but also chunks of Arizona, Kansas, Oklahoma, Texas, Colorado, and Utah.

Although Spain would control this vast chunk of land, most of it would not be settled by Spaniards. Much of this terrain would remain Mexico's wild frontier country that would more or less serve as a buffer zone, where Spanish and, after Mexican independence, Mexican troops would skirmish with Native American tribes, such as the Apache and the Comanche.

In fact, after Mexican independence, the Mexican Army found these two tribes so hard to deal with that they ultimately tried to bribe them in order to sue for peace. They did this by setting up "feeding stations," where rations could be handed out to tribe members. It sounds almost ridiculous to hand out food to an opponent so they do not attack you, but this was indeed the status quo for many years.

Tribes like the Apache and the Comanche thrived on conducting raids, as it was their way of life. The introduction of the horse only made them even more fearsome since they could raid a village and rapidly ride off with goods. Due to many years of skirmishes and struggles in the northern frontier, the settlers of Mexico settled upon this unique relationship to keep their livestock from being snatched and their family members from being killed.

It was largely only after the Mexican-American War, which had erupted in 1846, that this situation changed. After the conclusion of this war, the old Mexican northwest became the American southwest. It was then that the likes of Geronimo, the Apache warrior, would rise up as an incredible thorn in the side of the United States of America's Manifest Destiny.

Chapter 9 – The Conquest of Canada

"The advice I give to all adventurers is to seek a place where they may sleep in safety."

-*Samuel de Champlain*

Although Spain and, to a lesser extent, Portugal might have seemed as if they had a monopoly on the exploration of the Americas, they were not the only European explorers on the block. England entered into the picture as early as 1497, thanks to the skills of an Italian sailor named John Cabot, who worked for the English.

A map of what North America looked like in the 1700s. France, for the most part, held Canada and the western territories; Spain had the southern territories and Florida; and Britain's colonies stretched along the eastern seaboard.

Pinpin, CC BY-SA 3.0 <https://creativecommons.org/licenses/by-sa/3.0>, via Wikimedia Commons; https://commons.wikimedia.org/wiki/File:Nouvelle-France_map-en.svg

It has been said that after Cabot learned of Christopher Columbus's attempts to find a westward route to India, the wheels started turning in Cabot's mind. He relocated to England in 1495 and convinced English King Henry VII to finance England's own cross-Atlantic voyage of exploration. Cabot would set sail from Bristol, England, in May of 1497. He would then arrive in Newfoundland that June, claiming the land for England. The word "claim" here is very loosely used since although the claim was made, the English would not try to stake their claim until many years later.

Although this frigid northeastern section of North America did not seem to be rich in treasure like Mexico or Peru, Cabot and his men were amazed at how rich the coasts of Newfoundland were in marine life. They came back home with stories of the fish being so abundant in these northerly waters that all they had to do was dip a basket into the water, and it would come back up filled to the brim with fish. In later years, Newfoundland would become an enormous exporter of fish.

Cabot would embark on another voyage to North America in 1498, but somewhere along the way, disaster struck. Four of the five ships that took part in the voyage, including the one John Cabot was on, were lost. To this day, no one knows for sure what happened to John Cabot, but that was the end of his attempts at being an explorer.

England would soon become preoccupied with other matters. France tried to outpace England by utilizing another Italian mariner, Giovanni da Verrazzano. Considering the paths of Columbus and Cabot, which sent one south to the Caribbean and the other north to Canada, Giovani decided to take a route roughly in between.

His chosen course would take him right into the middle of the eastern seaboard of the future United States. In 1524, he landed in what would later become North Carolina.

The French, like the English, would soon become distracted by matters in Europe and put off further explorations. It was not until roughly ten years had passed, in 1534, that the French would send Jacques Cartier to explore the New World.

This time, the French expedition followed in the footsteps of John Cabot and made their way to Newfoundland. Jacques also explored the Gulf of St. Lawrence and even sailed to Prince Edward Island. They then traversed through Chaleur Bay, which is situated between Quebec and New Brunswick.

During this foray, the French came into contact with the Mi'kmaq people. The Mi'kmaq were friendly and ready to trade. They greeted the French by waving long wooden poles with furs hanging from the ends of them. This was an indication that they wanted to trade these furs. France would eventually take a lead role in the robust fur trade in North America.

As the men continued their expedition, the crew came into contact with one of the major players in this region of North America: the Iroquois. The relations between the French and the Iroquois were fairly solid, and Verrazzano even managed to capture a couple of the locals to take with him back to France. This, of course, was living proof of where the voyage had been and what they had seen.

Jacques Cartier was able to get further financing for more trips, and in 1535, he and his men made it back to North America, this time landing in Quebec. During this expedition, one of the explorers heard a local Iroquois calling the place kanata. This was an Iroquois word for "meeting place" and was a general reference to a place where people met.

The French, however, took it as the name for the land and soon were calling huge chunks of North American territory "Kanata" or, as it would become better known, "Canada."

This French expedition secured friendly relations with the local Iroquois of what is now Quebec, leading to the start of a bustling fur trade. The French enjoyed receiving valuable furs produced by the Iroquois, and the Iroquois appreciated the steel objects and other goods the French traded for them.

The Iroquois and French seemed to get along well enough, and for the most part, the French were able to travel freely through much of the Iroquois territory. During one of these forays, Cartier ascended a large hill and called it Mount Royal. In time, this name would morph into the term for Quebec's future city of Montreal.

Interestingly enough, since the French, just like the British, Spanish, and Portuguese, were still very much interested in finding an alternative sea route to East Asia, Cartier began to explore the St. Lawrence River for a waterway to China. He actually became convinced that there would be a way to navigate the St. Lawrence all the way to the East. In fact, the French referred to this part of the river as the Lachine Rapids. As silly as it might sound today, that is French for "the China Rapids."

Of course, Cartier was wrong in his estimation. There was no way he would be able to traverse a river in Quebec and somehow end up in China. There was a huge breadth of land still to traverse just to get to the Canadian side of the Pacific Ocean.

Nevertheless, the French exploration and conquest of Canadian territory would continue. Cartier would leave Canada in 1536 but come back in 1541, pretty much picking up where he had left off. He was still unable to find the fabled Northwest Passage, but he found boatloads of quartz and pyrite (sometimes called fake gold).

Although Cartier was an esteemed explorer, he was apparently no mineralogist, for he was convinced he had found large quantities of diamonds and gold. Needless to say, Cartier and his whole expedition became something of a joke by the time he returned to France. The phrase "as false as a Canadian diamond" even became a common expression.

Nevertheless, France would soon get a new champion in the form of Samuel de Champlain, who showed up in the St. Lawrence Valley in 1603. Samuel de Champlain would then push into Nova Scotia and establish the French colonial outpost of Acadia. However, French plans would soon be slowed down when England suddenly revived its interest in overseas expansion, beginning with the eastern seaboard of North America.

Chapter 10 – The Conquest of the Eastern Seaboard

"What dependence can I have on the alleged events of ancient history when I find such difficulty in ascertaining the truth regarding a matter that has taken place only a few minutes ago and almost in my own presence!"

-*Walter Raleigh*

Although the English got an early start at exploration with John Cabot, they long delayed following through and capitalizing on their gains. Queen Elizabeth I of England proved pivotal in getting the ball in motion. Queen Elizabeth wanted to make sure that England remained competitive with other European powers, and establishing overseas colonies was of vital interest to the queen.

She commissioned the explorer Walter Raleigh, who ended up establishing a colony in the Carolinas called Roanoke. This settlement was established in 1585; however, it would mysteriously come to an end. To this day, no one is quite sure what might have befallen the settlers of Roanoke. There are theories that they were killed by local inhabitants or that they even abandoned the settlement to live with the locals. Life in the colony was a struggle, so the settlers were vulnerable to attack or desired to desert the colony for a stable life elsewhere.

It was not until Jamestown was established in 1607 in the future state of Virginia on the eastern seaboard that things really began to take off as it pertained to English conquest and colonization. The colony of

Jamestown led to the establishment of a larger English colony: the Colony of Virginia.

Jamestown, like its predecessor, Roanoke, faced hard times. Many colonists would not survive. It is said that out of the original number of colonists, only about a fourth of their number would get to reach a ripe old age.

One of the more interesting stories (and one that is still open to question) to come from this period is the account of how the leader of the colony, Captain John Smith, came to interact with the local indigenous people. It has been said that when the settlers were on the verge of starvation, John sought the aid of a local tribe. He was supposedly taken prisoner and presented to a native leader named Chief Powhatan.

According to later accounts, Smith was about to be executed when the chief's daughter, Pocahontas, supposedly jumped in front of John Smith and pleaded with her father to spare his life. This would spark the romantic legend of John Smith and Pocahontas, which has had many fictionalized accounts (including a blockbuster Disney film) made in its honor. It is a nice story, but no one today seems to know how true or accurate any of it really is.

At any rate, Smith eventually made his way back to the colony and managed to secure food so that the settlers would survive.

From an economic standpoint, the British colonies on the eastern seaboard just did not seem all that profitable. All of the other European colonies had a way to generate revenue. Brazil had its sugar crops, Mexico and Peru had their gold and silver, and French Canada had plenty of fish and fur.

So, what did Virginia have to make colonization worthwhile? Well, the colonists found out what Virginia had to offer when they began to experiment with tobacco plants. Yes, tobacco, a crop that came to Europe's attention during the Columbian exchange, proved to be well suited for Virginia's climate.

Also in 1607 (the year Jamestown was founded), another colony farther up the eastern seaboard in what is now Maine was established. This colony was known as Popham Colony, but it was yet another English venture doomed to fail. Food was not in abundance, and the hostility of the locals made permanent settlement too difficult at this early stage of the English conquest.

The English would also add the island of Bermuda to their colonial fold. In 1609, an English vessel was blown off-course and sent crashing into a reef near Bermuda.

The crew spent some time on the island, weathered a bad storm, and managed to build a couple of new ships. These ships, christened Patience and Deliverance, would take most of the crew to their next adventure, but a few men opted to stay on the island. These few brave souls laid the groundwork for the start of an English colony, preparing the way for further waves of English settlers who would make the island a profitable enterprise.

Interestingly enough, Bermuda is one of the few overseas territories still controlled by Britain in modern times. Early on, the island was considered a part of the Colony of Virginia, and the island itself was dubbed "Virgineola." This name was changed to the Somers Isles, but most continued to call the island by its previous Spanish title, Bermuda.

The warm and comfortable island was soon full of English settlers and slaves. In Bermuda, as was the case in the rest of the Colony of Virginia, tobacco proved to be the big money maker, and soon this cash crop was being grown all over the island.

Another milestone in English colonization occurred in 1614 when Captain John Smith of Jamestown visited the old site of the Popham Colony in Maine. He was happy about the conditions he encountered in the region and decided that it would be a great place for some of the Protestants who were eager for a new land where they could practice their religion freely. This would lead to Protestants leaving England in September 1620. They headed to a part on the East Coast of what is now the United States of America on two ships—the Speedwell and the Mayflower.

However, the Speedwell was not all that speedy, and after filling up with water, it had to be scuttled. This meant the Mayflower had to be crowded with people, most of whom were Pilgrims. Those on board the Mayflower first sighted land off the coast of Cape Cod in the modern-day state of Massachusetts, which was in the vicinity of Plymouth Harbor, on November 9th, 1620.

This group of Pilgrims had been promised land by their backers, the Virginia Company of London. The Virginia Company had promised them land in the vicinity of the Hudson River. But it was cold, and winter was rapidly descending, so the settlers decided to stay where they were at Cape Cod.

Just prior to landing, the group established what would be called the Mayflower Compact. This compact was essentially a set of rules, a social contract that established what was expected of those who would come to create a new community in this small corner of the New World. Being fervent Protestants, the rules were understandably immersed in the Christian beliefs of those who wrote them.

The people on the Mayflower had a bit of a better go at things than those in Jamestown. The locals seemed to be more friendly than was typically encountered farther down the eastern seaboard. Instead of threatening the settlers, the locals seemed inclined to help them. This was evidenced when a local Native American man (likely from the Patuxet band of the Wampanoag tribe) named Squanto aided the settlers during a particularly harsh season by showing them how to plant the hardy crops found in North America, such as beans, squash, and corn. These crops would then sprout up as soon as springtime arrived.

It is believed that the Thanksgiving story of Pilgrims and Native Americans coming together to harvest bountiful crops and have a good meal is derived from these early encounters. Squanto not only personally aided the settlers but also introduced them to the local leader, Chief Massasoit. Massasoit was friendly enough, but he had some ulterior motives in aiding the settlers since he wanted to enlist them as allies to do battle with rival tribes.

Plymouth Colony was not making much money and was quickly becoming a drain on its financial backers in London. In order to mitigate some of this rampant debt, many of the colonists began to seek to earn revenue through fishing and engaging in the fur trade in the hopes that they could at least break even when it came to the expenditures that they were racking up.

Another settlement—the New Hampshire Colony—was set up in 1623. The colonists there were fairly successful when it came to fishing, with the settlers casting rods and setting nets up and down the coasts of what are today the states of New Hampshire and Maine.

These colonies on the northeast coast of the future United States would become known collectively as the colonies of New England. A major commonality among all of these settlers was their shared faith.

Many of them belonged to a particular strand of Protestantism known as Puritanism. The Puritans originated from England and had gotten their name from their detractors, who scoffed at how the adherents of this new brand of Protestantism were seeking to "purify" the Christian religion of perceived faults. The Puritans also developed a great sense of thoroughness as it pertained to their efforts to colonize the eastern seaboard of the United States.

The settlers believed they had a common bond due to their shared beliefs. This bond was so strong that the Puritans would not stand for anyone deviating from the rules and religion they had developed. While this might have provided some much-needed structure and solidarity in the early days of colonization, it would also create some terrible moments in colonial history. For instance, this strict and stringent environment led to something called the Salem witch trials. For those who are unaware of this event, the Puritans launched fiery accusations against those they deemed to have gone astray, which would lead to people being burned at the stake as witches.

Much of the English colonization of the Americas did break down along religious lines. In contrast to Spanish colonization, which was all Catholic and thus backed by the Catholic Church, in what would become the United States of America, various colonization organizations were formed, and all of them typically espoused one variant of Protestantism or another. The Puritans in New England and the Quakers in Pennsylvania are just a couple of examples of this.

However, English Catholics were not left out completely when it came to settling in the New World thanks to England's Lord Baltimore, who, after being granted a charter in 1632, set up a Catholic haven in the Maryland Colony. The English would then add the Colony of Connecticut a couple of years later, in 1636. This would then be followed by the Colony of Rhode Island, which was established that same year. Delaware would be founded in 1638, Carolina in 1663 (this would later split into North and South Carolina in 1712), New Jersey in 1664, Pennsylvania in 1681, and finally Georgia in 1732. Thus, England, which, through the Acts of Union in 1707, transformed into Great Britain, established its dominance of the eastern seaboard of North America.

However, the Colony of Virginia, thanks to all of its tobacco, proved to be the real money maker. England's colonization of the island of Barbados in the Caribbean in 1627 added the lucrative cash crop of sugar to the financial menu so that even more revenue could be recouped.

In 1648, more tropical island territory was claimed when a colony was established in The Bahamas. Then, the Spanish seized Jamaica in 1655. Spain would ultimately acknowledge British control of the Jamaican islands after the conclusion of the Anglo-Spanish War and the signing of the Treaty of Madrid in 1670, which officially ended the war.

At any rate, expansion on the eastern seaboard would continue, and by the 1670s, the colonists were getting into frequent skirmishes with the locals. In 1675, the Puritans of New England warred with the Wampanoag and other tribes in King Philip's War. This conflict got its name from the English colonists' main antagonist, Chief Metacomet, who had been nicknamed King Philip.

This conflict pitted Chief Metacomet's Wampanoag confederacy against the colonists, and the devastation caused by the hostilities would be immense. Several settlements were destroyed, and many settlers were killed. The colonists were eventually able to put a stop to the attacks on their settlements but only through the help of building up alliances with the Pequot and Mohegan tribes.

The fact that such alliances had to be made once again demonstrates how, in the early days of the conquest and colonization of the Americas, whether Latin America or Anglo-America, the European newcomers were just one power player among many. And among these many competing tribes, there were times when they could cooperate and be friends, but in other instances, they would end up as foes.

The European settlers often had to pick and choose alliances with several tribes to make progress. It was not long before this system of alliances would actually result in conflict between one or more European powers, as well as their Native American allies. In 1702, this situation came to a head when England, France, and Spain became embroiled in a conflict known as Queen Anne's War.

This conflict was rooted in ongoing hostilities between these European powers in the wake of the War of the Spanish Succession. That war erupted in Europe after the death of Spanish King Charles II. Queen Anne's War, which received its name from England's Queen Anne, was the spillover that occurred in each of the respective European powers' colonial holdings.

English settlements in the Carolinas, which at that time stretched all the way to Georgia, were in combat with Spanish-occupied Florida. In the north, colonists in New England were duking it out with the French in Acadia, Quebec, and Newfoundland. One of the main fault lines of the conflict ran up and down the Mississippi River, where the British and French, along with their various Native American allies, fought for dominance.

The wartime theater that really proved pivotal was in the northeast, where the British fought the French for naval dominance. The protracted struggle ended with the two parties signing the Treaty of Utrecht in 1713. This treaty was favorable to the British, allowing them to seize French Acadia on the northeastern seaboard, which the British renamed Nova Scotia.

The British also obtained Newfoundland, which they had long had designs upon ever since Cabot landed there in 1497. These acquisitions extended the British colonial grip, giving Britain almost complete dominance up and down the eastern seaboard of North America.

Chapter 11 – From Sea to Shining Sea: The Taming of the West

"The Americans are in general the dirtiest, most contemptible cowardly dogs that you can conceive. There is no depending on them in action."
-British General James Wolfe

The Americans would eventually call the notion that it was simply fate that Anglo-Americans would stretch from the Atlantic all the way to the Pacific Manifest Destiny. Usually, when people think of this, they think of the push westward, of cowboys and pioneers pushing through western deserts and wilderness on the Oregon Trail. And, of course, this line of thinking is correct. But most people do not realize that the American push westward actually predates the American Revolution. The push from the eastern seaboard of British America into the west can be said to have begun under the guidance of Great Britain.

Soon after Britain secured most of the eastern seaboard of North America, the British began to look westward. In the aftermath of Queen Anne's War, the British obtained Nova Scotia and Newfoundland and found themselves staring westward at Quebec. Quebec—not Arizona or Montana—could be considered the first phase of America's westward expansion. In light of renewed hostilities with France in 1756, by way of the Seven Years' War, Britain was presented with the opportunity to seize French territory in the Americas.

The colonial component of that war would become known as the French and Indian War, which actually began before the Seven Years'

War erupted in the European mainland. Some, particularly those in North America, consider the French and Indian War an altogether separate war, although most consider it a theater of the Seven Years' War.

The colonial charge against the French settlers would be led by none other than a young George Washington. The reason the war was dubbed the "French and Indian War" was because both sides, as was the case during Queen Anne's War, utilized various Native American allies.

The British forces ultimately won this conflict, and the resulting Treaty of Paris in 1763 had France coughing up considerable territories in Canada. Spain also gave Florida to the Brits. The British had captured Cuba and the Philippines, and the Spanish desperately wanted those lucrative territories back. However, the French contribution was the most considerable. For now, Britain controlled Quebec and much of the rest of Canada. With this major French bulwark thus removed, a major impediment had been eliminated as it pertained to westward expansion. But British America would not be the one to do all of this expansion, of course. That would fall on the United States of America.

Without getting too terribly bogged down in well-trod history about how and why the Thirteen Colonies rebelled against their British taskmasters, let us just say that there was significant disagreement between American colonists and British authorities on how things should be done in America. The colonists cringed at the fact that Britain could write laws that would impact the lives of those in the colonies, yet the colonists themselves had seemingly no say in the matter.

Add to this the economic drain that the French and Indian War had on the British economy. The constant wars in Europe and abroad resulted in higher taxation being enforced in the British colonies.

Sick and tired of being overtaxed and under-represented, the colonists wanted their independence, and they were willing to fight for it. The Revolutionary War broke out in 1775, and by aligning themselves with Britain's former foe, the French, the American colonists were able to beat the odds and defeat the British.

With their independence secure, it was not long before the nascent government of the United States began to look toward its western frontiers and consider a little conquest and colonization of their own. They had stiff competition, of course. The Americans had to deal with the indigenous inhabitants who called the land home and did not want to move and also against what remained of the old Spanish Empire. There was also another European player that arrived on the scene at this point: Russia.

Many are quick to skip over this important aspect of American conquest, but the Russians were making some pretty serious inroads into North America by way of Alaska, with the first viable colony said to have been established in 1784. The Russians sailed east out of ports in Siberia and ended up in what, from a North American perspective, was the far northwest of the continent in Alaska. To be exact, the Russians landed in the Aleutian Islands.

The contacts the Russians made among the local Aleut tribe of Alaska allowed a robust fur trade to be established. However, the relations were not always so friendly. In the early phase of these endeavors, the Russians often had to fend off attacks from the locals. But through a mixture of Russian reprisals and incentives by way of useful trade goods, a truce was more or less established, and the Russian settlers were able to live in relative peace in their Alaskan colony.

On the other side of the globe, in the nation of France, some rather earth-shaking events were taking place. France had aided the American cause and helped to ensure an American victory against France's old foe, the British. This was largely a case of pure and simple vengeance on the part of the French government, which desired to get back at the British, who had so thoroughly humiliated them during the French and Indian War and the greater Seven Years' War. The irony of an absolutist king of France supporting the American colonists' effort to shake off the king of England is ironic on many levels.

But most ironic of all was the fact that the ideals that led to the American Revolution would come home to roost in France. The French people no doubt realized that if the Americans could shake off their king and live in a free and democratic society, then why couldn't they?

Exacerbating this popular discontent was the fact that France had nearly driven itself bankrupt by bankrolling the American Revolution. France had doled out significant loans to the American war effort, which proved pivotal to securing an American victory. It also proved pivotal in sparking the French Revolution because all of this generous financing proved to be a severe drain on the French economy. This, in combination with some other financial missteps, led to a severe economic decline in France. Although the average French subject likely did not understand all of the specifics of what was transpiring, the economic downturn was quite palpable when they went to the market.

Even if one was not an intellectual who pondered the ideals of the Enlightenment made real through the American Revolution, the fact that the price of bread was suddenly higher than one's daily wages was enough to get mobs of protesters out on the street. The momentum of this mob of malcontents gave the French intelligentsia something to drive forward the French Revolution. A mob of people stormed the Bastille and opened the door for a radical change in government.

Obviously, we are skipping over some of the finer details of this immense and incredibly complicated event in human history known as the French Revolution. But in brief, it was popular discontent with the monarchy coupled with a severe economic downturn. This event would set in motion a chain reaction that would affect France, Europe, and the Americas.

Due to the tumult of the French Revolution, the remaining French colonies would be knocked into chaos. The French colony of Haiti in the Caribbean would revolt in 1791 and officially declare its independence in 1804, becoming the first nation of what we now refer to as Latin America to do so.

During the Haitian Revolution (1791–1804), France would be in turmoil. The chaotic Reign of Terror descended upon the nation, with great fighting both inside and outside of France. It would take the strong arm of a totalitarian dictator to bring some sense of stability. This dictator was none other than Napoleon Bonaparte.

Although France was not exactly an ally of the United States at this time, and although the American position on the conflict in France was to maintain a cautious neutrality (with the exception, of course, that brief naval episode called the Quasi-War), Napoleon proved to be a great and unexpected boon to the United States.

Napoleon Bonaparte, with the audacious, ad-hoc decision-making for which he was so famous, decided that the remaining French colonies west of the Mississippi River, known as the Louisiana Territory, were too burdensome for France. He also wanted money to fight the British, which was a more immediate threat. Napoleon offered the Americans a deal. For a sum of just 15 million dollars, the United States could add some 828,000 square miles of territory. The United States government believed the deal was too good to pass up, so it agreed to make the purchase.

Napoleon was very much a conqueror in the classic sense of the term. Even though he was giving up claims in North America, he was rolling all over Europe, knocking out several major nations. Spain was one of the major dominoes to fall. The fact that Spain was suddenly occupied by France essentially decapitated Spain's authority in its colonies.

After the Napoleonic Wars came to an end in 1815, Spain tried to restore these lost dominions, but save for Spanish possessions in the Caribbean, it was largely a lost cause. Eventually, all of Mexico, Central America, and South America slipped from Spain's grasp. This, in turn, made the newly independent nations of Latin America much weaker and more vulnerable to encroachment by other powers, such as the growing United States of America.

And it was not long before the United States sought to take advantage of that fact. Throughout the 1820s, American settlers were pushing against their western frontier. But as they did so, they pushed the native inhabitants out.

For example, the modern-day state of Indiana used to be part of a much bigger chunk of territory in the United States that had simply been dubbed Indiana Territory. The territory was called this for the pure and simple fact that there were a lot of Native Americans (Indians) who lived there. Today, the states east of the Mississippi, such as Florida, Georgia, Illinois, and Indiana, have hardly any Native American population to speak of, at least in comparison to the days before the European exploration.

Thousands of Native Americans were forced to walk the Trail of Tears. Although the famous "Trail of Tears" was walked by the Cherokee, Choctaw, Chickasaw, Creek, and Seminole tribes, other tribes east of the Mississippi had their own version of the Trail of Tears.

After the infamous Indian Removal Act of 1830, whole communities of Native Americans east of the Mississippi and south of the Great Lakes were forcibly moved west of the Mississippi River and away from where European Americans were attempting to settle. This was all a part of the gradual push westward from the eastern seaboard.

Soon enough, there would be a full -drive right through the heart of the southwest by way of a direct conflict with Mexico. Known as the Mexican-American War, this conflict, which erupted in 1846, would result in the United States claiming a vast territory that would include future southwestern states such as California, Arizona, New Mexico, and Texas.

After the Mexican-American War concluded in 1848, the real drive westward would commence. This inexorable drive west would very briefly be interrupted by the Civil War, which broke out in the US in the 1860s. By the war's end, railroads were already snaking across the land from east to west. The effort to link the eastern coast to the western one was moving full speed ahead.

Oh, and that Russian colony in Alaska? That would soon fall into US hands as well. Widely known as Seward's Folly, in 1867, at the behest of US Secretary of State William Seward, the United States purchased Alaska from Russia for around seven million dollars. Many did think that Seward had erred and that the purchase of this cold and icy land was a big mistake.

But both due to the vast mineral deposits of Alaska and later security concerns with Russia and China, most today likely consider it well worth the purchase. US territory would be stretched even further when, in 1898, efforts were made by President William McKinley to acquire Hawaii.

To say that the United States acquired Hawaii is a vast understatement. One could argue that we see the most blatant example of the United States engaging in outright military conquest. It was not quite the same as the Spanish conquistadors of old who just strode in and started battling for dominance. The American operation in Hawaii had much more subterfuge than that, but it was a forceful acquisition all the same.

It all began when American agents helped to overthrow the indigenous Kingdom of Hawaii in 1893. In its place, they established a short-lived independent republic. This republic was annexed to the United States in 1898.

That same fateful year of 1898 saw the United States wage the Spanish-American War, forcing Spain to relinquish its last colonial toehold in the Caribbean. Although the US lived up to its promise to the Cubans by granting them the independence they craved, the US would seize Puerto Rico, which remains a US territory to this day.

The United States would also grab Spain's once prized Philippines in the East, although this territory, after suffering invasion and conquest by imperial Japan, would be relinquished in 1946 in the aftermath of the

Second World War. Yes, whether it was through war or by way of the mighty American dollar, Manifest Destiny, the vision of the US stretching from sea to shining sea, was indeed becoming a reality.

Conclusion: The Legacy of the European Conquest

The conquest of the Americas at its outset came as a great surprise. It was as much a surprise to those who suddenly realized they had a whole continent at their disposal as it was a surprise to the original inhabitants of that continent.

The surprise was arguably much greater for those on the receiving end of the conquest than it was for the Spanish, Portuguese, French, and British. The European conquerors, colonizers, and explorers learned as much as they could about the land of the Americas and the peoples who inhabited it, but it would take the indigenous inhabitants far longer to learn who these invaders were and what exactly they were up against.

The native civilizations typically operated under the assumption that the invaders were merely a small group of random visitors that would soon depart and go back to where they had come from. The Maya expressed this when the Spaniards first landed on the Yucatán Peninsula; they bid the Spaniards to leave their land and go back across the sea. They had no idea that the Spaniards were playing for keeps and planned to stay. The Aztecs did not think the Spaniards would be a lingering presence either.

Even as Montezuma was handing out gold prizes, he bid the Spaniards to leave several times. The Inca emperors of Peru likewise thought that if they handed out enough gold and silver to satisfy the foreigners' strange cravings, they would leave them alone. The Inca leader Manco Inca would come to the conclusion that this was not the case, as he bitterly lamented that even if all of the mountains of his realm should turn to gold, it would not be enough for the Spaniards.

The indigenous people underestimated the scope of the conquerors' greed as well as their intentions. They had no idea these strangers would eventually put permanent roots in their land. Eventually, more rugged explorers would arrive, as well as whole families that would introduce their own ways of life, religion, and systems of society.

The indigenous fur traders of Canada were likely equally surprised when the few rugged French fur traders they came into contact with to trade fur for steel pots and pans ended up bringing their families along for the ride. The same could also be said for the Anglo-American experience in colonies on the eastern seaboard, such as Jamestown and Plymouth. Many tribes were hostile to the newcomers, but some were friendly. But no matter what their disposition, none could have imagined that these meager outposts hugging the eastern coast of North America would one day expand until they covered a vast expense of territory reaching all the way to the western coast of the Pacific.

The awful reality would slowly sink in, punctuated by various tragic intervals of anguish, such as the Trail of Tears. Yes, it is always a sad legacy when one civilization conquers another. However, it is best to see these things for what they are and to face them head-on. As much as we might be tempted to view one side as monsters and the other as victims, conqueror and conquered alike were human beings who faced human problems.

For example, prior to Hernán Cortés's conquest of the Aztecs, the Aztecs were the most brutal conquerors on the block. They had conquered and subjugated most of their neighbors. The Tlaxcala, the Spaniards' later indigenous ally, were one of the few holdouts the Aztecs were unable to conquer. If the Aztecs could have lorded it over the Tlaxcala, they most certainly would have. If the Aztecs had ships to sail across the Atlantic and weapons far superior than any the Spaniards had at the time, the Aztecs likely would have invaded Spain. This is not an attempt to be a revisionist or to indulge in wanton speculation; this is just an acknowledgment that until very recent times, much of the world lived by the old adage of "might makes right."

Human nature almost always calls for some sort of excuse or rationale in these sorts of situations. It would indeed be rare (but not impossible) to find a historical account in which one group invades and assaults another with the official rationale given for the assault being, "We did it because we just wanted to hurt people and take their land."

Even though many might have these base instincts of hurting and stealing from others, they would most likely never admit it. Human nature almost always makes aggressors come up with some sort of excuse for their actions. In the early 1950s, for example, the Chinese launched a brutal and unprovoked invasion of Tibet. The communist government of China has engaged in a harsh occupation of the region ever since.

Yet, in the history books of communist China, the invading Chinese troops are presented as the "good guys." And they absolutely do not refer to their conquest of Tibet as a "conquest." In fact, it is officially referred to as the "liberation of Tibet." Liberation? Liberation from what? Well, the communist Chinese pat themselves on the back for supposedly liberating the Tibetans from their old ways of life.

The Tibetans still practiced feudalism at the time of the invasion, so the brutal invasion and occupation by communist Chinese is presented as Tibetan "liberation" from their feudal ways.

The conquistadors could very well have presented their conquest of the Americas as a kind of "liberation" of the native peoples from their ways of the past. And in many ways, that is indeed how the conquistador framed their actions in the New World.

No matter how much blood was shed and no matter how cruel the occupying troops might have been to the locals, it was chalked up as being part of the greater good, of "freeing" the locals trapped in the "darkness" of their pagan ways and shining forth the light of Christian beliefs.

It is a terrible thing to contemplate, but throughout much of history, it was the guy with the bigger stick who lorded it over the rest. Fortunately, in the 21st century, we seem to have largely moved beyond this terrible mentality (with a few notable exceptions). However, during much of the human experience, this heavy-handed domination by force was not the exception at all—it was the rule.

Here's another book by Captivating History that you might like

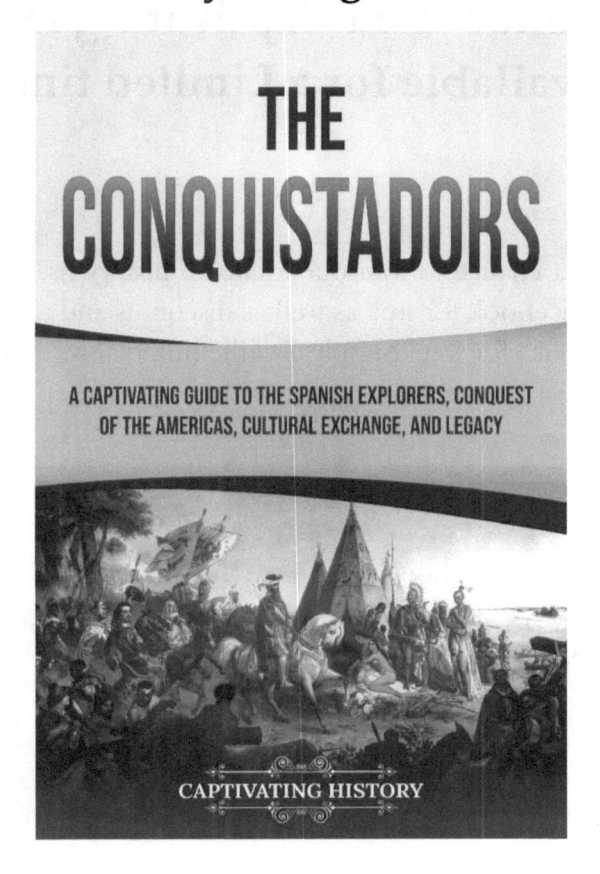

Free Bonus from Captivating History (Available for a Limited time)

Hi History Lovers!

Now you have a chance to join our exclusive history list so you can get your first history ebook for free as well as discounts and a potential to get more history books for free! Simply visit the link below to join.

Captivatinghistory.com/ebook

Also, make sure to follow us on Facebook, Twitter and Youtube by searching for Captivating History.

Appendix A: Further Reading and Reference

Disney, A. R. *A History of Portugal and the Portuguese Empire: From Beginnings to 1807 Volume I: Portugal.* 2009.

Fernández-Armesto, Felipe. *Our America: A Hispanic History of the United States.* 2014.

Foster, V. Lynn. *A Brief History of Central America.* 2007.

Koch, Peter. *The Aztecs, the Conquistadors, and the Making of Mexican Culture.* 2005.

Saunt, Claudio. *West of the Revolution: An Uncommon History of 1776.* 2014.

Stein, R. Conrad. *The Conquistadores: Building a Spanish Empire in America.* 2004.

Suranyi, Anna. *The Atlantic Connection: A History of the Atlantic World, 1450-1900.* 2015.

Wood, Michael. *Conquistadors.* 2000.

Made in United States
Troutdale, OR
09/11/2025